Strategies for the Threshold #1

Dealing with Python:
Spirit of Constriction

Anne Hamilton

with

Arpana Dev Sangamithra

Dealing with Python: Spirit of Constriction

Strategies for the Threshold #1

First edition © Anne Hamilton and Arpana Dev Sangamithra 2017

Second edition © Anne Hamilton and Arpana Dev Sangamithra 2021

Published by Armour Books

P. O. Box 492, Corinda QLD 4075

Cover Image: Walk in the Light by Graham Braddock

Interior Design and Typeset by Beckon Creative

ISBN (print): 9781925380637

ISBN (ebook): 978-1-925380-39-2

National Library of Australia Cataloguing-in-Publication entry

A catalogue record for this book is available from the National Library of Australia

All rights reserved. No part of this publication may be reproduced, stored in, or introduced into a retrieval system, or transmitted, in any form, or by any means (electronic, mechanical, photocopying, recording or otherwise) without the prior written permission of the publisher.

Please note: this book uses Australian spelling, punctuation and grammatical conventions.

Strategies for the Threshold #6

Dealing with Python:
Spirit of Constriction

Anne Hamilton

with

Arpana Dev Sangamithra

Scripture quotations marked BSB are taken from the The Holy Bible, Berean Study Bible, BSB Copyright ©2016 by Bible Hub Used by Permission. All Rights Reserved Worldwide.

Scripture quotations marked ESV are taken from the ESV® Bible (The Holy Bible, English Standard Version®), copyright © 2001 by Crossway, a publishing ministry of Good News Publishers. Used by permission. All rights reserved.

Scripture quotations marked "Darby" are taken from the Darby Translation Bible. Public Domain.

Scripture quotations marked GNT are taken from the Good News Translation in Today's English Version - Second Edition Copyright © 1992 by American Bible Society. Used by Permission.

Scripture quotations marked HNV are taken from the Hebrew Names Version of the Bible. Public domain.

Scripture quotations marked ISV are taken from the Holy Bible: International Standard Version®. Copyright © 1996-forever by The ISV Foundation. All rights reserved internationally. Used by permission.

Scripture quotations marked KJV are taken from the King James Version of the Bible. Public domain.

Scripture quotations marked NAS are taken from the New American Standard Bible®, Copyright © 1960, 1962, 1963, 1968, 1971, 1972, 1973, 1975, 1977, 1995 by The Lockman Foundation. Used by permission. (www.Lockman.org)

Scripture quotations marked NLT are taken from the Holy Bible, New Living Translation, copyright 1996, 2004. Used by permission of Tyndale House Publishers, Inc., Wheaton, Illinois 60189. All rights reserved.

Scripture quotations marked NIV are taken from the Holy Bible, New International Version®, NIV®. Copyright © 1973, 1978, 1984, 2011 by Biblica, Inc.™ Used by permission of Zondervan. All rights reserved worldwide. www.zondervan.com The "NIV" and "New International Version" are trademarks registered in the United States Patent and Trademark Office by Biblica, Inc.™.

Other Books By

Anne Hamilton

Devotional Theology series

God's Poetry: The Identity & Destiny Encoded in Your Name

God's Panoply: The Armour of God & the Kiss of Heaven

God's Pageantry: The Threshold Guardians & the Covenant Defender

God's Pottery: The Sea of Names & the Pierced Inheritance

God's Priority: World-Mending & Generational Testing

More Precious than Pearls:
The Mother's Blessing & God's Favour Towards Women
(with *Natalie Tensen*)

Mathematics and Theology in Medieval Poetry

Gawain and the Four Daughters of God:
the testimony of mathematics in Cotton Nero A.x

Award-winning Children's books

Many-Coloured Realm

Daystar: The Days are Numbered Book 1

Merlin's Wood: The Battle of the Trees 1

Contents

Introduction		11
1	**Python Piles on the Pressure**	15
2	**Python Goes to the Movies**	47
3	**Python Meets its Match**	61
4	**Python and Yoga**	91
5	**Python Goes Down for the Count**	103
Appendix 1	Brief Summary	149
Appendix 2	Random Stuff	153
Appendix 3	Common Symbols of Python	161
Appendix 4	*The Silver Chair*	163
Endnotes		181

Acknowledgments

I am indebted to so many people who have helped my thinking and who have shared their lives with me as I have journeyed through the threshold process.

However, in the making of this book, there are just a few people I would like to single out as having helped at crucial times:

Michael Knoeppel, who in checking the words in the Jewish language starting with the Hebrew letters 'peh' and 'tav', was instrumental in pointing out to me the relationship between Python's tactics and its name.

Ben Gray, who first drew my attention to the terms constriction and wasting, which so perfectly described the threshold experience.

Donna Ho, who provided first-hand information on what a 'Friend of the Court' in Australia entails.

Arpana Dev Sangamithra, who generously contributed almost all of Chapter 4.

Meredith Swift, Elizabeth Klein, Quang Hii, Natalie Tensen, Melinda Jensen, Janette Busch, Alison Collins, Rhonda Pooley, Judy Rogers and Janice Speirs who contributed a wide variety of valuable insights.

My mum, Dell Hamilton, who crafted the prayers at the end of each chapter.

The wondrous Trinity—Abba Father-God, Jesus His only-begotten Son and the Holy Spirit—without whose guidance it would be impossible to get out of the clutches of Python.

Introduction

PAUL OF TARSUS WROTE: *'...that we would not be outwitted by Satan; for we are not ignorant of his designs.'* (2 Corinthians 2:11 ESV)

True as that statement was some twenty centuries ago, it's not the case today. In so many ways, it's a pity this book is necessary. However, so few believers are aware of the tactics of the enemy of our souls, it seems timely to collect the information outlined in *God's Pageantry* and *God's Pottery* in a more systematic way.

This book focuses on one of the most common of all threshold issues: a sentinel spirit known as Python.

I can't say I enjoyed pulling this together. CS Lewis said once in an interview: 'Of all my books, there was only one I did not take pleasure in writing... *The Screwtape Letters*... They were dry and gritty going... making goods 'bad' and bads 'good' gets to be fatiguing.' I relate to his feeling: after writing about Python for a while, I felt almost suffocated and desperately wanted to write something about the loveliness and majesty of God.

As usual, this book is meant to be the opening of a discussion—not the last word on the topic. As usual too, it's designed with a mathematical underpinning, a numerical literary style inspired by the word-number fusions of the gospels and epistles.

Importantly, I sound a note of caution to all readers. I have noticed that, whenever preachers are writing or speaking at length about spirits like Python, then the particular spirit under consideration shows up in the teacher's words about three-quarters of the way through their presentation.

I have prayed that *absolutely nothing* in this book should ever be construed as an invitation to Python to be present in these pages. Nevertheless, should you discern something amiss in any wording, please contact me—because it's a matter I certainly do not wish to go unaddressed.

Throughout this book, the terms *threshold* and *threshold covenant* will be used constantly. As far as the word *threshold* goes, whenever it is used in a spiritual sense here, it denotes the entry point into our destiny. It's essentially the 'doorway' or the 'opening' into the individual calling God has appointed for each of us before the foundation of the world. As for *threshold covenant*, the concept is re-introduced, after a long period of historical obscurity, in *God's Pageantry* and *God's Pottery*.

One of Scripture's shortest books is Jude. It doesn't mention Python or thresholds, yet alludes to them constantly. And it finishes with this assurance of God's protection:

> *Now unto Him who is able to keep you from falling, and to present you faultless before the presence of His glory with exceeding joy, to the only wise God*

our Saviour, be glory and majesty, dominion and power, both now and forever. Amen.

Jude 1:24 KJV

If I have one recommendation before you begin this book, it's this: read Jude. Closely and carefully.

Lastly, please note: I love the fiction of CS Lewis, author of *The Chronicles of Narnia*. I once tried to read his poetry but gave up after the first page, deciding he'd been wise to move on. However, in trying to understand the symbolism of the dreams my sister and I had as children, search engines repeatedly led me to the work of 'Clive Hamilton', a name which turned out to be a pseudonym of Lewis. I went back and persisted through that poetry—only to realise he knew much more about familiar spirits than he'd ever said. I was angry. I felt I needed to know what he'd kept secret. It's only *after* you understand the nature of threshold and name covenants you can see how his fiction deals with the relevant issues. It both conceals and reveals at one and the same time.

Yet now—nearly two decades on—I understand his reticence. If God doesn't give you permission to pull aside the curtain on His secrets, then you don't. Now, Appendix 4 on *The Silver Chair* is not for everyone. It is long, rambling and wordy—and not quite in keeping with the rest of the book. But somewhere in the world, there are a few individuals who need to know what's in it.

Anne Hamilton

July 2017

1

Python Piles on the Pressure

THE LAST STEP, THE FIRST step, the boundary, the frontier, the gateway, the door, the bridge—there are so many different ways to picture thresholds. Our ancestors considered such liminal places to be dangerous and fraught with risk.

In taming so much of our world, we've largely forgotten how perilous a threshold really is. Only a few places still remind us: the hazardous cross-currents of an ocean bar, the wild turbulence of the sound barrier, the pain and unpredictability of giving birth. All of these difficult transitions in the natural world testify to a spiritual reality: thresholds are intrinsically unsafe. They can never be taken for granted.

And because, deep down, we know this, many of us choke on the last step. We can't cross the line into the new or out of the old—and our own inability baffles us.

A colleague of mine went to a theme park and decided he was going to take on the challenge of the highest diving platform there. He climbed up the mega-high tower all the way to the — *second-last* step. And there he froze. No matter what his brain said to his feet, they refused to move. His muscles rejected his self-talk that it was just another step. He couldn't get his legs to obey his mind's instructions. Eventually, because he simply couldn't make it onto the top of the tower, he dived off the second-last step. 'The difference,' he said in telling this story, 'between the final two steps was nothing compared to the height of the tower. I've never been able to understand why I was paralysed at that moment.'

The fact is: a last step, like a first one, constitutes a threshold. It may not be a spiritual threshold but it's a physical one. And the natural always clues us in to what is happening in the spiritual. So often our hearts know what our minds fail to recognise: *all thresholds are exceedingly dangerous.*

Precisely as our ancestors said they are.

Although the spirit of Python isn't the only sentinel stationed on a threshold, it's the one we usually recognise first. It's a constrictor: it tries to squeeze us so tightly we feel forced to surrender to its agenda. Its goal is to block us so that we are never able to access our divine calling.

Our English word *python* is actually related to one of the Hebrew words for a *threshold*. It's probable that *python* is directly related back to 'pethen', an ancient Jewish word meaning *cobra, asp* or *adder*.[1] Moreover 'pethen', this word for various venomous serpents, is also the origin of the Biblical term 'miphtan'—a word that specifically denotes not just a threshold, but a *defiled* one.[2]

It's clear from this relationship between 'miphtan' and 'pethen' that the Hebrews recognised Python as a threshold guardian. Now it happens that Python is explicitly mentioned only once in Scripture (in the Greek wording of Acts 16:16); however, its presence should not be overlooked whenever 'miphtan' appears in the text.

More subtly, Python often rears its head when words for *choking* or *strangling*, *doorways* or *gates*, *openings* or *stumbling-blocks* appear at critical moments in Biblical history. Various literary hints show it was the zeitgeist—the 'spirit of the age'—during the period of the Judges. Most significantly, it makes several anonymous appearances in the life of Jesus—its identity only shown by distinctive words or the signature descriptors in its behaviour.

Python doesn't work alone. It is part of a cabal of spirits—that is, a focus group conspiring together to achieve the downfall of God's plans for your life. Its especial interest is the threshold into your calling. In part, this is because it is a fallen cherub originally charged with guarding spiritual entryways. The gifts of God being irrevocable, it still retains that high office, though using it to ruthless ends.

Before looking at why Python is able to hold on to so much power, let's look at its modus operandi.

The primary tactic Python uses to achieve its agenda is **constriction**.

Finances, time, health, appearance, qualifications, education, position, reputation, personal circumstances, work situation, racial background, availability of resources, personnel or networks—there are many ways Python can constrict our ability to enter into our calling but the most obvious is lack of money.

When money is the issue, we look around for partnerships or financial backers. We search for someone we can trust to help us *complete* our calling. But when Python is present, we often discover many people want to *compete* with us instead.

When thresholds are involved, Python has a right to be there—striking at our choices.

My brother was just starting out in plumbing design when he got talking with a friend about an idea he had to revolutionise water pumps. 'I'd like to help you!' the friend said. 'I'll be your backer.'

They discussed the innovation and various requirements for building a prototype. However, life soon got in the way for both of them. The day-to-day business of earning a living became a natural priority and mutual availability of time became another source of **constriction**. Nevertheless, they agreed together to pursue the idea as soon as they could both carve out enough time to put a genuine effort into it.

A year later, my sister-in-law was watching the televised finals of the Young Inventor of the Year competition. She realised that the brilliant idea my brother had had for a pump had just won top prize. The prize-winner? The son of my brother's friend.

My brother's **constriction** became his friend's opportunity.

When Python is involved—and it always will be on a threshold—the outcome can never be predicted. You may think a friend's character is utterly impeccable and absolutely beyond reproach—but, until that moment when he raises his heel to cross the threshold, you don't know whether he will raise it *against* you. Or not.

Because it is a unique moment. And he doesn't know either.

Caroline was an elegant, but overweight, woman with impeccable taste in clothes. After many years in a government department, she felt the call of God to go into a ministry of preaching and teaching. Quitting her long-term career in the public service and sacrificing the security and pension it entailed, she enrolled in a Bible College. For three years, she topped the academic results.

Towards the end of her final term, she was called up before the accreditation board for an interview. Her hopes were high for an appointment in a prominent church. But they were not only dashed, she was crushed by the board's devastating pronouncement: because of her weight, she would never be offered any position in that denomination.

'Crushed': it's one of the words that people use when Python is operating. If you listen to the choice of language, you'll soon begin to detect the presence of this spirit.

Caroline's story also highlights Python's second tactic: **silence**. Before Caroline enrolled, she should have been informed her weight was a barrier to ordination in that denomination. But for three years, no one even hinted it was a problem. At the last possible moment, when it was too late for her to do anything, she was told of a hidden criterion she could not have suspected.

Silence is also an aspect of my brother's friend giving his son a leg-up into starting out in business by appropriating the idea for the innovative pump. Silence is often accompanied by **ambiguity**.

'You are our preferred candidate,' Tom was told by the board of selectors at a major university. He was flown internationally at the selectors' expense, shown around the campus for a week and given a temporary office. He took part in major discussions within the department and contributed valuable insights. He felt he fitted perfectly into the collegial atmosphere.

He went home, assured of the position. He and his wife both put in notice at their respective jobs and began readying their children for the move. Meantime, specific questions in his emails were going unanswered. His attempts to phone and clarify issues were frustrated. Unable to make contact with the right people, he became worried and anxious. He'd been told that, as soon as his appointment was approved, he'd receive a contract. But the time for a new term was fast approaching and it hadn't eventuated. In the meantime, he was in limbo.

The day before term started, Tom received a text message to say the position would be re-advertised. As he looked back in disbelief on all that happened, he realised no one had ever said the job was his. Just that he was 'the preferred candidate', and that 'as soon as your appointment is approved, you'll receive a contract'—in retrospect, an extremely ambiguous statement that told him the condition for receiving a contract but didn't actually guarantee it.

The final outcome was in such contrast to the effusive welcome Tom had received he was shattered. 'The last two weeks of complete silence,' he said, 'were like slow strangulation.'

'Slow strangulation': again, the language reflects an instinctive knowledge of the spiritual dynamic in play. *Strangulation* is a good word to associate with a constricting, squeezing entity like Python.

'Worry' is another one. *'Worry'* in actual fact comes from a German word for *'strangle'*.

Ambiguity is, by its nature, very hard to spot. When people frame their responses so that they have possible double meanings—just in case wriggle room is needed—it's deceit. Lawyers may have schooled them on subtle, slippery words that won't come back to bite them. But the fact is: anyone who practises **ambiguity** regularly will lose the trust of family, friends, colleagues and clients very fast.

We can save our skins one way, only to lose something more important: our reputations.

There is a way to pick up on **ambiguity** as a deliberate ploy. It should be considered as a possibility when *exactly* the same wording is repeated in different conversations. Most of us aren't lawyers or experts, intent on the accuracy of our wording, so in conversation we tend to be loose in our terminology.

And strange as it may seem, truth can generally be expressed in a variety of ways and words.

But **ambiguity** can't be. It isn't trying so much to be true as *not false*. Precise wording is needed to achieve this kind of subtle deceit: so the phrasing tends to be exactly the same each and every time.

People don't have to watch their words when they are telling the truth. But they have to guard them very carefully if they are trying to be ambiguous.

～

Python's tactic of **silence** is a very effective and efficient one. People use it to avoid conflict while, in some cases, they are rethinking their position. But this very lack of transparency will rupture relationships if they decide *for* themselves, and *against* others.

Silence, when it is used as a ploy, simply comes down to keeping certain information secret that should be shared. It's ignoring the words of Jesus: *'Do to others what you would have them do to you.'* (Matthew 7:12 NIV) It's leaving unsaid things that become more damaging every moment they are left unsaid.

But there's a related ploy. Sometimes the two are used in conjunction with each other. This second ploy is silencing.

Silencing is about shock tactics. The silence is broken with such lightning speed or such stunning, unexpected words that those on the receiving end are stupefied. They don't know what to say. They're in disbelief, reeling from the surprise blow. So they're silent. Not because they want to be—but because they have absolutely no idea how to respond in a loving, truthful way.

It may take hours or days to formulate the right response. And by then, it often feels too late. *L'esprit d'escalier*[3] is the term borrowed from French for this predicament of thinking of the perfect reply too late.

Many people decide that the right moment to say the right thing has long since passed—and so they decide to never say anything. They've been silenced.

Caroline was silenced. She didn't know what to say or do. Years later, she sought healing through prayer ministry when the pain simply wouldn't go away.

Silence and **silencing** are Python's tactics to ruin lives. For those maintaining silence or practising silencing, it's a blip in their mental landscape as they get on with living. Now they're setting themselves up for a major fall later on—Python may be their temporary ally, but they've sauced themselves up as a meal for the spirit of backlash, Leviathan.

The most complex issue surrounding silence is, however, for the onlooker. The person who is not the active decision-maker but who has privileged information about their intentions. The observer who knows that the decision-maker is maintaining silence about their objectives.

Python wants those observers on-side. It tempts them into silence as well. The temptation is a subtle one and can take various forms. Python will reassure the observer that silence is not a lie; it will point out that speaking may violate a confidence and indeed be a betrayal; it will remind us that it's possible to needlessly ruin a reputation and that breaking the silence is not, in fact, our responsibility; and it will plant in our minds the seductive thought that forgiveness and silence are often the same thing.

This is an even more insidious trap. It's often rigged as a double-bind so that, whatever choice observers make, someone will be betrayed. Whatever we do, we'll be in complicity with Python. That might seem a harsh assessment but, when it comes right down to it, if our silence puts another person in harm's way or in the path of temptation, we are potentially assisting unholy spirits of the threshold in another's downfall.

And that's a matter for repentance, just as it is for those actively involved and not merely looking on.

Until the moment Caroline came along, the question of 'suitable appearance' probably hadn't ever crossed the minds of the members of the accreditation board. But Python made it an issue.

Until the moment my brother revealed his idea for an innovative pump, his friend had probably never considered advantaging his son by betraying another person. But Python made it a possibility.

Python brought up a new, previously unconsidered choice—a choice that was probably unthinkable in the past: to sacrifice a friendship for the sake of securing his son's place in the business world.

In that story it's important to note there is more than one threshold. One was my brother's and one belonged to the son of his friend: both were at the beginning of their careers. What my brother's friend almost certainly would never have done for himself, he was not only enticed to do for his son—he actually succumbed to the temptation.

When Python is active, we're lured into doing for people we love the very things we'd never do for ourselves. And we're silent, as we begin a mental exercise to justify as well as hide our actions.

But when we're the target of the **silence**, we have a slow-growing sense of anxiety, culminating in a feeling of betrayal. In fact, Python's ploy of **silence** often tempts people on the receiving end to fall for its third tactic: **divination**.

After I put up a Facebook post on the methodology of Python and its use of **silence**, a woman I'd never met contacted me to ask for prayer. She'd had a fight with her fiancé several days previously and he'd stormed out. She'd tried phoning, texting and emailing but he was silent.

She felt as if her heart were being squeezed tight by a boa constrictor. So my Facebook post on the spirit of Python had deeply resonated with her.

I messaged back, 'Yes, it sounds like Python. And if it really is, you might well be tempted by the silence into divination. When you're unsure of what to do next and God seems to be silent too, you can be enticed into fortune-telling. Even if that's as simple as opening your Bible and plonking down your finger to see if there's any guidance in the verse you touch.'

She was so grateful. 'Just minutes before I saw your message, I had looked up the phone number of a clairvoyant,' she wrote. 'I know that sounds a terrible thing for a Christian to do, but I am so desperate.'

She went on to testify that **divination** was a repeated temptation: 'I've done that—asking for God to reveal the truth and opened the Bible at random. I see how that is very much magical thinking. Interestingly enough though, it was this very act—me desperately grieving and wanting answers; in fact, I considered seeing a psychic but dusted off my Bible instead—that led me back to God. The verse my eyes fell on was very, very specific about the dangers of divination and warning His believers to stay away from it. I've only used the random-verse method when I feel led to and always asked God to be in charge. But I'll repent and never do it again, certainly... and be grateful God kept me safe all those years ago.'

Divination is a counterfeit of prophecy.

The difference between the two is not always obvious since, in both cases, there's a proclamation of future events. **Divination** is the practice of attempting to foretell future events or discover hidden knowledge by occult or supernatural means. It is powered by Python while prophecy is powered by God.

In fact, **divination** is so intrinsic to this spirit's nature that many translations of Acts 16:16 do not actually name Python. They choose to describe one of its functions instead and call it 'the spirit of divination'.

This name avoidance wouldn't have mattered much to the ancient Greeks who would have immediately identified it anyway, since they understood **divination** to be a gift of Python Apollo. This god presided at the oracle at Delphi—where possibly the most famous Sybil of the ancient world practised fortune-telling and soothsaying.

Now Python wants to tempt us into **divination**. It particularly wants to tempt anyone who has a calling to the office of a prophet into this unholy arena. The purpose of **divination** is to know the future and, with that foreknowledge, to choose expediently in the present. **Divination** is about acquiring the knowledge to position yourself to the greatest possible advantage as the future unfolds.

Prophecy, on the other hand, is only incidentally about the future. To the prophet, the future is not fixed immutably. The prophet can shape the future. For the Hebrews, prophecy is about understanding pattern—it is about forth-telling, not foretelling. It is about speaking the future based on a knowledge of God and His Word.

In saying a prophet can 'shape the future', it is more subtle than simply the power of a prophetic word coming to pass. It is about recognising the pattern, realising how the particular pattern will outwork in personal, corporate or national life, then going before God in His council to negotiate with Him on behalf of others. This is why so much prophecy in Scripture is a call for repentance. A prophet can 'shape the future' by drawing attention to the need for change and, if that change occurs—as happened, for example, when Jonah preached at Nineveh—then God will withhold the destruction He has planned.

Or, if He will not, then in His mercy He may modify its timing. Jesus tells His followers about a coming day of judgment and says: *'Pray that your flight will not be in winter or on the Sabbath.'* (Matthew 24:20 NLT) The Day is appointed—in the sense that God has decreed it will definitely happen—He won't be persuaded by an Abraham, a Moses or an Amos. However its date is not set in concrete. Praying believers can influence its timing.

Repentance may delay the Day—as so often happened in Israel's history. Solomon, Hezekiah and—perhaps surprisingly—Ahab all repented, and God delayed judgment and justice as a result.

But you won't find any mention of repentance when it comes to **divination**. The future is fixed, not negotiable.

In Hebrew, just as in Greek, **divination** is connected with a serpent. Hebrew 'nachash', *to practise divination*, is the same word as 'nachash', *serpent*.

The confusion between **divination** and prophecy has meant many believers are lured into crossing the line from faith to magic. But the answer is simple: go before God and repent.

Many people say you don't need to know the name of a spirit to deal with it. Others think exactly the opposite: that you should demand to know its name. Some ministers go further still: they insist that the spirit should manifest itself in some way.

Now if a spirit does manifest spontaneously, that's one thing. However, I personally feel that such a command is unnecessary and often dangerous. Moreover, depending on wording and attitude, it may violate a biblical injunction to do so.

As for knowing its name, I prefer that to be the case: not so I can have power over it—which is one of the greatest mistakes and temptations it's possible to fall into—but so its secondary agendas can be discerned.

If people's language indicates the presence of Python—when words like *squeezed, squashed, choked, pressured, crushed, tightened, strangled, constricted, suffocated* and *throttled* are used—then it's possible to warn them about its wider tactics. Just to know there will be a lure into divination because of the silence, the uncertainty and the ambiguity helps us stand against that particular temptation. Just to know it is Python and not, for example, Leviathan, informs us the next set piece in the constriction process is likely to be intimidation or seduction and that's incredibly helpful.

To be able to recognise a tactic for what it is often enables us to stand firm in resisting Python's demonic programme. We can be praying about the tactics even before they happen. We can already have positioned ourselves to call on God for His help the moment any specific strategy of this entity becomes evident.

Python is one of the fallen cherubim. The significance of this is that, as we approach a threshold, it is entitled to check us out for *righteousness*. Rachab, the spirit of wasting, is another of the fallen cherubim and also checks for *righteousness*. Leviathan, on the other hand, is a seraph and is looking for something entirely different.

Now, way back at the gates of Eden, God stationed the cherubim and armed them with flaming swords to prevent the unrighteous from entering the garden. So, herein is the nub of the problem as we encounter Python while attempting to pass into our calling: *'There is none righteous, no, not one.'* (Romans 3:10 KJV)

Python will only allow the righteous to pass. But none of us are.

All is not lost at this point. Python will actually allow faith to be credited as righteousness (in accordance with God's word as in, for example, Genesis 15:6). However, it will do everything in its power to cause that faith to fail.

Everything.

Not everyone falls for Python's ploy of **divination**. However, it has a fourth tactic to bring down your faith: **intimidation**.

Coercion, threats, bullying. Terror, if necessary. Whatever duress it takes. The purpose of any brutal assault is to lead you into doubts about yourself and your calling as well as doubts about whether you can trust God.

Such coercion doesn't even have to be extreme to achieve its purpose.

Jan had worked with some street-kids for months, using her flair for drama to perfect a theatre production which incorporated a Gospel presentation. With the help of her husband, she'd taken the show on a regional tour. The finale had been an acclaimed evening's performance in their own church with over a thousand people attending.

They were elated to see the growth in the kids they were mentoring. The morning after the performance they were asked to see the church's senior pastor. Jan was still on a high after the buzz of the previous evening and thought the pastor was going to discuss a commissioning service for their work. She believed he intended to publicly bless their efforts with the street-kids and talk about opportunities to expand the outreach.

Instead, to their incredulity and dismay, he asked them to give up the theatre troupe entirely. Not only that, he requested all the work with the street-kids be discontinued. He wanted Jan and her husband to devote their time to overseeing the church's Sunday School.

Shocked but obedient, they sacrificed what they thought was their true calling—just as they believed they'd finally come into it.

As they said later, they didn't feel they really had a choice. They believed in honouring authority, and that became Python's point of coercion.

We see higher-level techniques of pressure and intimidation in Scripture when Moses sent twelve spies into the Promised Land. During this significant threshold time, they encountered three giants—the sons of Anak—and ten of them became so scared they forgot God had fought for them against Pharaoh and his armies.

Python is more than willing to call up its spiritual allies if it senses it's losing. It may summon help from Leviathan, the spirit of retaliation, or from Rachab, the spirit of wasting. However more commonly, it sends for the spiritual equivalent of the three fearsome giants who evoke doubt: the sons of Anak who so intimidated ten of the spies as they scouted the Promised Land.

The name Anak is instructive: it means *the one who chokes, the one who strangles, the one who throttles.* Yes, the power behind the giants was certainly Python.

The tactic of intimidation generally works well against us. It certainly worked well against the Israelites—so well they spent another 38 years in the desert.

And then, on the threshold of the Promised Land once more, they had to face Python yet again. This time its guise was Baal Peor, *the lord of the opening.*

With the advent of Baal Peor, the spirit of Python trots out tactic number five: **seduction**.

The enticement can be sex. But it needn't be. Power, prestige and position can all be dolled up with a glamorous veneer to present a virtually irresistible object of desire. And if your price isn't any of those, perhaps it's love, intimacy, security. Or simply someone to stave off loneliness.

Now the Israelites were almost finished their wilderness wanderings when Python slithered up for the second time. Almost an entire generation of males had perished—only Caleb and Joshua were left of the age group who voted for Python and not God when they were last on the verge of the Promised Land. This new generation had learned to trust and lean on God for survival for almost four full decades, so the tactic of **intimidation** was no longer a realistic option.

It was time for Python to unpack something different. Arriving on the west bank of the Jordan River, the people camped in the Valley of Acacias. Perhaps it wasn't the wisest choice of location—this was the ancient site of the Cities of the Plain—Sodom, Gomorrah and their satellite towns. Truly the people should have known better than to pitch their tents in that long-defiled landscape. The Hebrew word for acacia is related to *turn aside*. That was the message of the valley: *go elsewhere.*

But they didn't. And, arrayed in their tribal units, they were observed from the heights above by the king of Moab and his court. With the king was the diviner Balaam from Pethor.

'Pethor' is related to 'pethen', *python*. Pethor is variously translated as *opening, prophetic utterances* or *interpret dreams*[4] and was long considered to be the site of an oracular temple. For centuries it was synonymous with the Jordanian city of Petra. However, this identification has been disputed in recent years.

Balaam's reputation as a seer transcended borders. An international superstar of the ancient world, he was hired by King Balak to curse the people of Israel. On the way to perform this task, he was almost killed by a sword-wielding angel and was only saved by his quick-thinking donkey. Somewhat ironically, this donkey turned out to be an oracular seer surpassing Balaam himself.

It took a while but Balaam eventually got God's message that he was not allowed to curse the Jewish people. His employer, King Balak, was decidedly unimpressed when not once, but three times, Balaam delivered prophecies of prosperity for Israel. So unimpressed was Balak it's clear that, had Balaam not held a sacred office of diviner and dream interpreter, he'd have come to a nasty end then and there. Eventually he did come to a nasty end, but not at Balak's hands.

After offering sacrifices to Baal Peor while surveying the massed tribes of Israel but failing to curse them, Balaam effectively disappeared from the foreground of the narrative in the Book of Numbers. Much later it's revealed that, to get his pay from the king of Moab, he counselled Balak to beguile the Israelites into idolatry so that God's protection would be removed from them.

This is the purpose of **seduction**. To lure you out from under God's protection. To entice you away from the shelter of God's covering. To expose you to the flaming arrows of the enemy.

Not surprisingly, the Hebrew words for *seduction, enticement* and *lure* along with associated concepts like *opening yourself to seduction* are all close relatives of 'pethen', *python*. So too, amongst others, are *twisting, winding, riddle, pretence, excuse, suddenly,* and *surprise* along with *wick* and *engraving*. A few minute's reflection on these words will show how they fit with the activities of Python. *Engraving* might be tricky without knowing a threshold stone is engraved. *Wick* may be difficult too without knowing it is a *twisted* thread; in fact, the English word, *wicked*, comes from this notion of twisting.

Now when it became clear to Balaam that God was never going to break covenant with His people, the only option was to get them to break covenant with Him.

There's a simple reason for this. Covenants entail automatic curses for breaking them—and if God intervened to stop those particular curses, He'd violate His own word. If He is indeed a God of truth, He has to keep *His* vows. And since those vows involve curses for violating covenant, His protection would equally have to be lifted, if the Israelites broke *their* vows.

Our ignorance of Scripture enables Python to manipulate many modern concepts of grace. Unknowing, unsuspecting, we fall into the error of expecting God to violate His own word.

This particular tactic of Python was an immense success. Some local princesses were sent in to seduce the Israelites and it didn't take long before many of the men were engaged in ritual prostitution. The purpose of such prostitution is to 'become one' with the god—in this case that deity was Python's alter ego, Baal Peor, *the lord of the opening*.

Now the purpose of covenant is actually to 'become one'. Therefore ritual prostitution is a counterfeit of covenant. In 'becoming one' with Baal Peor, the Israelites forfeited Yahweh's covenantal protection over them.

They 'stumbled', they 'fell', they 'dashed their foot against a threshold stone'. Revelation 2:14 NAS spells out a parallel sin: *'you have there some who hold the teaching of Balaam, who... put a stumbling block before the sons of Israel...'*

The error of Balaam is additionally mentioned in Jude 1:11, *'...they have rushed headlong into the error of Balaam,'* and 2 Peter 2:15, *'Turning out of the true way, they have gone wandering in error, after the way of Balaam.'* In every case, it's about enticing Christians to leave the cover of God's protection so they will be smashed—not so much because a high-ranking spirit has attacked them, but as an upshot of ignoring the clearly stated consequences in God's word.

Both Jude and Peter outline what will happen if you dishonour spirits like Python—yet many believers attempt to use the covering of the blood of Jesus to neutralise these Scriptures. This is effectively magic: the use of God's design for redemption in a purposeful attempt to cancel out God's word. And of course, the use of magic simply deepens our opposition to God.

Seduction opens the way for tactic number six. Actually, it's not so much a tactic as a consequence: debilitating **illness**, chronic disease, plague.

The Hebrew word for plague, 'maggephah', comes from 'nagaph', *strike*. This is consistently used to describe the action of refusing a covenant by striking or dashing a foot against a stone.

The action of striking a threshold stone denotes a refusal to accept a covenant that has been offered. Plague broke out because, in breaking covenant with God, the people lost His covenantal defence. In effect, God said, 'You're on your own now. You've chosen Baal Peor, you've voted with your feet for Python, so let it protect you.'

Rather than God sending the plague that ravaged the people, it's more accurate to say He withdrew the guard keeping it at bay.

Python's ultimate goal is to bring you to a point where God's protection is withdrawn.

Rick was just finishing up his postgraduate studies when he was offered his dream position. He was invited to go into partnership in a fledgling start-up company in another country. He was thrilled beyond words because he knew it was a God-given opportunity. He'd been involved in a mentorship with his prospective partner and knew they'd make an unbeatable team.

Of course, there was a sacrifice to be made—that goes without saying. However, Rick was willing to pay the price involved: he'd have to move overseas.

He sold up. His apartment, his car and his truck. He gave away his furniture, television and sound system, his refrigerator and even boxes of books. He was determined on a clean sweep. A new life, a new beginning.

Throwing over the final semester of his postgraduate university studies, he gave in his notice at his workplace and refused three plum job offers in the month that followed.

His excitement mounted. On the night before he was due to fly out, he celebrated by taking all his friends out for a farewell dinner.

They were in the middle of a set of mutually complimentary speeches when his phone rang. He took a moment to look at the text. It was from his new partner. 'Don't come,' it said. 'I've decided to go it alone.'

Rick threw up.

His world was shattered. He'd been replaced in his workplace, none of the three job offers he'd received were still open, his qualifications for other jobs were less than adequate because he'd chosen to throw in his post-graduate studies. Replacing the goods he'd sold or given away seriously dented his savings and, six months later, he was in dire trouble. Worst of all, his relationship with God was shredded.

What had happened to all the personal promises he felt God had made to him?

Now Python's ultimate objective is achieved if it can get you to ask this question and come up with no answer. Are you going to fully trust God the next time you approach a threshold?

No. Almost certainly not.

Keith Butler tells this story:

'I was fired from only one job in my entire secular career, and it was through no fault of my own. This particular job was a union job in which after you work for 90 days, you become a member, and they can't fire you. But they can fire you any time from your first to your 89th day on the job.

'For my first performance review, I received a good evaluation. For my next review, I got a promotion. Then, based on that review, they granted me the transfer I requested, to a better position with the accompanying higher salary.

'Then the regional boss, who had the power to override everyone in command at my office, fired me on the 89th day! Remember, I would have become a member of the union the very next day. I had just received a promotion and had received nothing but glowing performance reviews.'[5]

The remainder of his story points out that God works all things together for good. But let me mention that this event has Python's signature all over it: the lightning strike at the last moment. Just as in Rick's story, Python all too often waits until the last possible moment—when you're on the cusp of victory and you least suspect it—to inflict maximum damage with a lightning strike.

In fact, this tactic is so much a speciality of Python that I've sat in prayer ministry with people, querying them repeatedly about the significance of the day—or the day after—the attack occurred. Sometimes it's only been through adamant insistence that they rack their memories that it's been possible to uncover what threshold they were about to cross when the assault happened.

Commonly it's the very last day that Python chooses for its strike.[6] With more time, you might be able to regroup from your state of disarray and shock—but there is no time.

And this leads you on inevitably to the 'if onlys'.

Constriction.

Silence. Ambiguity.

Divination.

Intimidation.

Seduction.

Illness.

Along with illness, Python often combines an additional element: **torment**.

'If only': *if only* the boss would give me a break; *if only* I'd married someone else; *if only* my friends would loan me the money; *if only... if only*.

'What if': *what if* I had the opportunities my parents did; *what if* I had more influential friends; *what if* I had a better education; *what if... what if*.

'If' is a word that invites Python into any situation. Assuming, of course, it's not already there. And 'if' can't always be avoided. It's not meant to be a cue word for **torment**, but when we go into that mental space, we've turned from God. We are no longer trusting that His plans for us are good; we're no longer believing He is keeping our future safe in His hands.

In Rick's case, Python didn't have to get past its second tactic, **silence**, before it was ready for the kill. His example also illustrates what every situation with Python is going to involve: the demand for a **sacrifice**.

It's the instinctive gut-level knowledge that every threshold requires a sacrifice that caused my colleague to freeze on the second-last step. That knowledge of a need for sacrifice caused Caroline to turn aside from her dream of ordination, instead of fighting the system; Jan and her husband to abandon their work with street-kids and fall in with their pastor's request; Rick to give away what he couldn't sell.

My mother saw an advertisement for a hostess to meet and greet new residents coming into our suburb. We'd just moved to a different area, much closer to my dad's workplace. The suburb at the time was just a few streets and houses—but it was growing very fast.

When she inquired, she discovered the job entailed delivering welcome baskets and informing the new arrivals about local amenities and services. It was perfect for her abilities, talent and personality.

So she applied. There was a long and complex interview process, an IQ test, a training period. She sailed through it all with flying colours. In fact, she was later to say that she realised she was genuinely intelligent for the first time when her test results came through.

But, in the end, she didn't take the job. The day before she was to go out into the community with her first welcome basket, she resigned.

There was one aspect to the job she didn't find out until that day. The position was, in part, funded by an insurance company who wanted reports assessing the wealth of new arrivals by observing the possessions in their homes. My mum felt she was being asked to spy and, in addition, being asked to sacrifice her integrity.

The timing was, of course, designed to try to ensure she didn't have enough time to consider her options and couldn't back out. If you look back on my brother's story or Tom's, Jan's, Rick's or Caroline's, you'll find this same aspect: the demand for sacrifice or the revelation you are the sacrifice is timed to cause maximum damage financially, mentally, emotionally or spiritually—and sometimes all three.

Once you are committed beyond the point of no return, Python is able to wreak uncontrolled havoc. And its work is done.

Paul wrote:

> *'...we would not be outwitted by Satan; for we are not ignorant of his designs.'*
>
> 2 Corinthians 2:11 ESV

Unfortunately—unlike Paul—we *are* ignorant of the satan's schemes. Very dangerously so. We don't see Python's overarching plan. It's not simply a spirit of constriction or of divination. We therefore need to understand the most common ways it sets itself against us. It's important to get a feel for both its overall agenda as well as the finer details of the process.

Because even as we overcome it, Python doesn't leave cleanly. It has a final cloying corruption to throw behind it as one last defilement for us. It can raise a stench of **jealousy**. We can become inexplicably jealous of others; or they can become inexplicably jealous of us.

We don't have to experience all these issues to identify Python as the source of our problems. The fact is: most of us give up or give in long before even half of its campaign is over. Python's aim is achieved when it forces us to choose between two things: either back off from the threshold entirely or make the sacrifice it demands.

It would prefer the sacrifice rather than to watch us withdraw. Because if we make a sacrifice, we are offering it worship. We are also trading with it for the privilege of entering the doorway into our calling. This creates a much more toxic spiritual dynamic—instead of fighting Python with all our might, we've now joined it. With that sacrifice, we've given our allegiance to the kingdom of darkness.

How is this possible? Trading is, in actuality, a counterfeit of covenant. So when we sacrifice to Python, we partake in a false covenant. And because covenant is primarily about 'oneness',[7] God withdraws, declining to be one with us while we're one with a spirit of divination, intimidation, constriction and seduction.

Let's take a moment to pray before we look further at how this diabolically clever entity operates.

However, even before that, let me sound a note of caution.

I strongly recommend that the following prayer and, for that matter, all the prayers in this book are read through carefully before being prayed aloud with intentionality. If you feel a check in your spirit from the Holy Spirit about any aspect of the prayer, then heed it. Put off the prayer until you receive permission from God.

It is vitally important to recognise that prayer is about relationship with the Father. It is not intended as a formula. The prayers in this book are meant to be guidelines to help you realign yourself with the holy Trinity; they are nothing in themselves; they are meant as a starting point, not an end in themselves.

Transformation is only possible as you hold onto the hem of Jesus' prayer shawl and ask Him to mediate before the Father for you. In the end, it's all about Him!

Prayer

Abba Father, as I've read these tactics of Python, I realise how many of them I've fallen for.

I've been duped by the counterfeits; tempted by the baits; taken—and been taken by—the lures; frustrated by the constriction; wounded by the torment.

I ask that Your banner over me is love as I confess my faithlessness to You. My head knows that You always remain faithful to me regardless, but my heart has wavered so long that I'm only just clinging on.

I am now aware that Python requires a sacrifice and has enticed me to achieve my destiny by sacrificing Your honour, my own integrity or another's advancement. I've chosen to fall in with its schemes. My ignorance is no excuse for my behaviour.

When I rejected You, I also rejected Your protection and covering. I ask Your forgiveness and pardon. I speak out my forgiveness to those who have sacrificed and dishonoured me and I ask Jesus, through the power of His blood and His cross, to empower my words and give them authority in the spirit realm to achieve Your will for them.

Abba Father, my choices have left me exposed and unprotected. Please be my one and only safe refuge. Sharpen my mind and my senses so that I am more alert to Python's tactics. Open my eyes to its deception, subterfuge and trickery so that when it tries to attack,

I can run to you as my safe tower and refuge. So often when I am on the verge of stepping into my destiny—the destiny You gave me even before my conception—I feel I am being strangled. I know it is Python testing me, demanding my surrender. Abba, grant me the grace to move back under Your covering, remain there and never negate Your blessing again.

Holy Spirit, hover over me and speak to my heart in ways that I understand so I can stand firm against Python. Thank you Abba, Jesus and Holy Spirit for your protection and love.

In the name of Christ. Amen.

2

Python Goes to the Movies

A SWIRL OF BLACK CLOAK, a dramatic flourish of martial music, a fade to slow, heavy breathing. Darth Vader strides into the *Star Wars* universe and, in his opening scene, lifts a rebel officer off the ground by his throat and proceeds to squeeze the life out of him. 'Force choke', it turns out, is a favourite death stroke of this Dark Lord of the Sith.

Throughout *A New Hope*, Darth Vader continues to play a threshold guardian role reminiscent of Python. The fact that his name was Anakin Skywalker before he fell to the dark side doesn't detract in the least from the Python symbolism. Rather, it enhances it. The biblical giants of Hebron who were Python's agents and who intimidated the spies reconnoitring the Promised Land were called 'Anakim', sons of *Anak*.

In the critical scene when the hero and the villain first come face to face, threshold symbolism abounds. Luke Skywalker is heading for the *Millennium Falcon*, about to make good his getaway from the Death Star along with Han Solo, Princess Leia and Chewbacca.

He comes out the door leading to the deck where the spacecraft is docked. Here's the first overt threshold symbol: a doorway.

Darth Vader appears just beyond another doorway. Second overt threshold symbol: the giant guardian at the gate; third overt symbol, of course, the gateway itself.

Vader and Obi Wan then engage in a light-sabre duel. During this fight Obi Wan deliberately sacrifices himself. Here is the fourth overt symbol: the sacrifice on the threshold.

Of course, there are other symbols in the background: it has already been established that Darth Vader is not just any threshold guardian, but specifically python-like in nature because of his use of 'Force choke' as well as his monstrous appearance.

George Lucas framed the *Star Wars* saga around Joseph Campbell's theories of the 'Hero's Journey'. A significant element of Campbell's work examines the perilous encounter with the threshold guardians.

Society at large may have forgotten Python—but movies haven't.

Tyler Durden in the morally ambiguous cult film, *Fight Club*, sets up a threshold test for anyone wanting to participate in Project Mayhem. All the applicants are rejected initially as too young, too old, too fat, too thin, too whatever. But if they stand on a dilapidated porch for three days and nights without food, shelter or encouragement, they're allowed in.

'Tyler' is a name like 'Anakin'. Just as 'Anakin' evokes a threshold guardian through its likeness to 'Anakim', so 'Tyler' has similar mythic and spiritual connotations.

Tyler, Tiler, Taylor, Tailor and all their variant spellings come from the same late Latin root, meaning *to cut*. That meaning alone links it tangentially to covenant, since we don't *make* a spiritual covenant, we *cut* one. But the direct relationship of the 'tiler' to the cherubim comes about through Masonic ritual. The 'tiler' of Freemasonry—and similar organisations—is charged with standing at the threshold to protect the Lodge from enemies within or without. His sword is supposedly ceremonial: actually, it's to kill anyone who is a threat to the Lodge.

The original guardians of the threshold were the sword-wielding cherubim who guarded the gates of Eden. In fact, 'cherub' and 'chereb', *sword*, rhyme in Hebrew.[8]

Tyler is a name so deeply entangled with the idea of threshold that, when it is given within a family, it's indicative of a generational struggle with Python. It's also symptomatic of ungodly covenants within the family line including, but not limited to, the vows associated with Freemasonry.

Parents give such names unconsciously—some instinct draws them to a name that highlights the long-term family problem and puts a cry for divine help in front of them every single day. Every time a parent speaks such a child's name they are:

1. naming the unresolved issue in the family line
2. presenting it before the Lord for His aid

3. prophesying to the chosen one he will actually settle the problem, cleanse the generational stream and mend the world.

Many films use the idea of threshold guardians who eventually become the hero's allies. One movie to use this trope is the *Princess Bride*: the hero Westley encounters a trio of testers in Vizzini the Sicilian, Fezzik the giant, and the swordsman, Inigo 'You-killed-my-father-prepare-to-die' Montoya.

Here are aspects of both the Anakim and cherubim: the threatening giant and the incomparable sword-wielder.

But there the resemblance ends. Python will never turn into an ally while you're refusing to sacrifice to it. And should it turn into an ally because you've sacrificed to it and covenanted with it, then God will withdraw. The shelter of His wings, His covenantal protection and His presence as a strong tower will be gone.

In addition, while Python *may* be your ally—a situation far from constant and assured as time goes on—you've set yourself up perfectly for retaliation by Leviathan.

Thresholds come in many guises: gates, doors, bridges, borders, shores, embankments, cliffs, limits, edges, beginnings, endings.

In the aptly-named *Monty Python and the Holy Grail*, the concept of the terrifying threshold guardian is adapted from the ancient Greek myth of Oedipus meeting the Sphinx. But the movie gleefully satirises this time-worn trope. Instead of a hybrid creature with the body of a lion and the face of a woman,[9] the Grail-seekers from Arthur's court are met by a rag-tag old man at the entrance to a bridge.

Three seemingly innocuous questions are put to the knights. After Sir Robin and Sir Galahad fail to respond appropriately to the old man, they are pitched into a volcanic abyss. King Arthur is left to face the guardian's next question: 'What is the air-speed velocity of an unladen swallow?'

Arthur, puzzled, wants clarification. 'An African or European swallow?'

With a question for a question, the tables are turned. The guardian, unable to answer, is himself catapulted into the abyss.

Movies have remembered a spiritual reality our culture has otherwise forgotten. Threshold guardians exist—and the ungodly ones are unremittingly hostile.

Turning from movies to literature, the finest example anywhere of the modus operandi of both Python as well as the other threshold spirits is the classic children's fantasy adventure, *The Silver Chair*. This is the ultimate exposition of what threshold covenant is all about. It's so detailed, in fact, I consider it an inescapable conclusion that CS Lewis must have known all about deadly constriction and wasting first hand.

Internet statistics repeatedly declare that he experienced 800 rejections before he sold a single piece of writing. Now many experts consider this number utterly unlikely, if not a complete fabrication. After all, his first collection of verse was published when he was just twenty years old.

Still, it can be accurately said that Lewis never achieved his true ambition. He always wanted to make his name as one of the great poets of the twentieth century, not as a novelist. That dream continually eluded him.

Despite this, I'm sure many people would think my assertion he experienced deadly constriction and wasting is exaggerated, if not totally false. Surely the fame resulting from his *Broadcast Talks* and his best-selling books, *Mere Christianity* and *The Chronicles of Narnia*, should negate the thought. How could Jack Lewis genuinely know anything about constriction and wasting?

Well, it's unprovable of course but still I can't see how anyone who hasn't experienced the full gamut of threshold conflict could portray the spiritual dynamic as intimately and comprehensively as he does in *The Silver Chair*.

The reason it goes unnoticed is because most people are entirely ignorant of the existence of a threshold covenant, let alone its characteristics. So we miss seeing this portal fantasy for what it really is. In fact, it was only as I came to write down a list of defining features of a defiled threshold that I noticed what Lewis had done.

Here's my list. As you align yourself to take up the calling which you sense God has purposed for you, you experience most, if not all, of the following:

1. a sense of a doorway into destiny
2. attack by the spirit of forgetting
3. attack by Python, the spirit of constriction and divination
4. attack by Rachab, the spirit of wasting
5. attack by the spirit of rejection
6. attack by a vampiric spirit
7. attack by an army spirit
8. silence on the part of those who could help your decision-making
9. ambiguous information from those you encounter
10. intimidation by giants
11. seduction into ease and comfort
12. an unconscious urge to sacrifice to the threshold guardians
13. a need to deal with the writing on your personal threshold stone
14. a choice to pass over the threshold or to trample on it
15. the tendency to think 'If' or 'If only'
16. spiritual seals that are related to your own name and its covenant

Writing them down in a list like this makes it seem like we face huge, insurmountable odds. In fact, we do! But just as Eustace and Jill in *The Silver Chair* overcame giants and evil enchantments simply by obeying

Aslan's directions, we too can tackle powerful cosmic entities through the grace of God and holding on to the hand of Jesus.

As it happens, the characters who symbolise the vampiric spirit and the army spirit in the book are not, despite their appearance, threatening in any real way. The story (see Appendix 4) actually drills down to focus almost entirely on Python. In the climatic scene, Eustace and Jill come to the aid of the kidnapped Prince, whereupon the formerly sweet and comely Lady of the Green Kirtle transforms into a massive python. She then tries to crush Prince Rilian to death.

He has already destroyed her engine of sorcery: the silver chair which held him captive and took the memory of his true self from him for all but one hour a day.

I have to wonder what that silver chair of the title really symbolised for Lewis. His surname was Welsh, despite his Irish upbringing and his English schooling. And, for the Welsh, a 'silver chair' had a very particular meaning: it was the coveted prize awarded to the top bard in an eisteddfod. It was the way a poet's gifts were recognised and accorded the highest honour.

So was the title really about the destruction of Lewis' long-cherished ambition to be lauded as a poet? Did he come to see in that aspiration an enticement by Python to forget his true gifts and calling?

It's impossible to be sure—but I believe the author was laying his ambition on the altar even as he wrote this story.

When the truce was agreed and Arthur was ready, he said to his knights, 'Be wary and watchful, for I trust not Mordred. If you see any sword drawn, come fiercely forward, and slay the villain and his guard.'

Mordred gave the same warning to his lords, for he had equal mistrust of Arthur, whom he feared and doubted.

The two leaders now advanced and met between their armies. But by a fatal chance, as the king and his opponent were in consultation, an adder came from a heath bush and stung a knight on the foot. Feeling the wound he drew his sword in thoughtless haste to kill the venomous serpent.

But the instant the armies on both sides saw that sword flash in the air all was uproar and tumult. Like two mighty waves of battle the great warhosts broke from their stations and rushed together across the plain.

Adapted from *The Sting of the Viper*
The Romance of Reality, Historic Tales Volume 14
Charles Morris

And so Camelot ends. The romantic realm, the kingdom of courage and justice, the dream-like utopia of later ages, all screeches to a halt with the bite of a viper.

Python again: we see it sometimes in slow constriction and other times in the lightning strike. We see it at the beginning of an enterprise and at its tragic ending. We see it in words like *adder* and *viper,* along with *cobra* and *python*—all English translations of the same Hebrew term 'pethen'.

Throughout our common heritage of literature, we find a memory of Python as a deadly threshold spirit continually lurking below the surface.

The movie, *King Arthur: Legend of the Sword*, borrows indiscriminately from the wide corpus of Arthurian romance. It uses motifs from ancient Celtic poetry, throws in a pinch of French medievalism, nods briefly to various modern retellings—then proceeds to dish up a mythic offering on the nature of thresholds. Every last threshold spirit appears in some form in the movie—even, to my great surprise, the one I've dubbed the 'Janissary'.

Python makes its appearance as a sinuous water-dwelling fiend. It reminds the evil king, Vortigern, that his arcane power comes from a covenant—with a price to be paid. The sacrifice is costly to an almost unfathomable degree—it has to be someone the king loves.

The movie is permeated with the concept of threshold sacrifice. It's not simply about good and evil in medieval costume, it's about the choices both Arthur and Vortigern face as each approaches different liminal moments. Arthur consistently chooses self-sacrifice while Vortigern has no problem sacrificing others and indeed, at several points, revels in it. These choices—the sacrifice of self or the sacrifice of others—are the two most common options Python presents to all of us on the threshold.

Arthur's mythic Camelot is not the only kingdom that ended in the flash of a serpent's strike. The vast empire of Egypt fell to Rome when Cleopatra allegedly committed suicide with the aid of an asp. Her name *glory of the fatherland* can also be translated *keys of the fatherland*—and, with her death, the keys did indeed turn and the door open for Roman occupation of vast new territories.

Alexander the Great was at the gates of India, on the verge of his greatest triumph, when he fell ill with fever. The last to attend him at his deathbed were Seleucus, a general, and Peithon, his bodyguard. Peithon means *python*. In the division of Alexander's empire amongst his generals and friends, Peithon became satrap of Media, such a vast and strategic section it was recognised it would be possible for him to destabilise the entire empire. He was compelled to give half his holdings up. His name is not the only one it is possible to associate with a threshold. Ptolemy, the general who received Egypt and Judea in the carve-up of the territory conquered by Alexander, is also a contender.

The imposition of the Greek language on the subjugated peoples had far-reaching effects. Greek became the lingua franca of the time—and remained so for centuries. As a consequence, Hebrew was no longer universally spoken in the Jewish Diaspora—and the Scriptures were translated into Greek, the 'Septuagint', to accommodate this new challenge.

Now Ptolemy was the first of a line of rulers ending with Cleopatra—and both names in my view are indicative of historical thresholds. Python is at play in subtle ways, even in their names. Ptolemy, quite apart from starting with the letters *pt* (see Appendix 2)—is derived, in my view, from the same root as Talmai, one of the sons of Anak, the agents of Python.

Throughout our literary heritage as well as the historical record, the evidence is in: at threshold moments, Python is there in some form or other. Yet when we face our own personal call into destiny, we don't want to acknowledge its presence. We assume that, because we're responding to God's call, nothing can touch us. We consider our particular situation sacrosanct—totally devoid of this particular spirit. Some of us think that, if we ignore Python, it'll go away.

But it won't. It has legal rights to challenge us. But before looking at that, let's examine how Jesus and Paul both interacted with it.

Prayer

Yahweh Perets, Lord of the Breakthrough, and Jesus of Nazareth, Door of the Sheep, I ask You to provide me with the cover I need to cross over the threshold into my destiny. I ask You to come swiftly as my strong protector whenever you warn me, through signs and symbols, through dreams and visions, through everyday events, through what I watch and what I read, that Python is coming to test me.

The spiritual life is not nearly as simple as I've wanted to believe. Python is a spiritual reality I've faced and I admit I have not overcome it. It has legal rights to test and tempt me. My bad choices as I've succumbed to its subtle temptations have caused havoc and destiny malaise in my life.

I acknowledge my need of Your help to be constantly on guard against its many tricks and ploys and I acknowledge my need of Your strong protection and wisdom to make Godly choices to stand firm. Forgive me for trying to overcome Python in my own strength. I repent of any and all times I used my own wisdom, relied on divination or was seduced out from under Your covenantal defence.

Help and heal me, Yahweh Perets.

In the name of Jesus, the Door of the Sheep. Amen.

3

Python Meets its Match

THE ONE AND ONLY TIME the spirit of Python is mentioned by name in Scripture is in Acts 16:16.

> 'And it came to pass as we were going to prayer that a certain female slave, having a spirit of Python, met us, who brought much profit to her masters by prophesying.'

This verse is taken from the Darby Translation. Other Bible versions are quite different. Very few English translations actually mention Python—some use the phrase *spirit of divination*; some choose *soothsaying* or alternatively *clairvoyance* or *fortune-telling*. These words obscure the original Greek: 'Python'. Granted that one ploy of Python, as we have seen, is to lure us into divination. However, that's just one aspect of its overall agenda. It's not the totality.

These descriptions—*divination, soothsaying, clairvoyance* and *fortune-telling*—are valid ways to indicate the presence and activity of Python. Still, they have an unfortunate effect. For most readers, they are eminently reassuring and carry an unwarranted soothing quality, implying that, unless believers are hanging around fortune-tellers or mediums, they're extremely unlikely to encounter Python.

But Python's presence is not dependent on the company we keep, though obviously it's a factor. Python features in this story because it's a threshold event.

Let's look at the details more closely. Paul and Silas[10] were in the Greek city of Philippi and, for several days, had been followed by a slave girl while they were making their way to prayer. She'd been shouting, *'These men are servants of the Most High God who have come to announce to you the way of salvation.'*

Eventually, despite the free advertising, Paul turned on her and cast out the spirit. As a result, the owners of the slave girl—incensed at losing the profit she earned for them—dragged Paul and Silas before the magistrates. They were beaten seriously, then thrown in a dungeon. Then, while they were singing praises at midnight, an earthquake occurred and the prison doors flew open. The jailer, thinking the inmates had escaped, was about to kill himself but stopped on hearing Paul's voice. Subsequently, he and his entire family were saved.[11]

Almost every preacher focuses on the climax—the conversion of the Philippian jailer—with the praises at midnight a close-run second in the spotlight. The incident is so isolated from the wider context of Paul's ministry that the fact he was in the process of crossing a major threshold when he encountered Python is completely obscured.

Philippi wasn't just another whistle-stop town on one of Paul's missionary journeys. It was the beginning of something new. The Spirit of Jesus had blocked Paul's way into Asia and he'd subsequently had a vision of a man of Macedon calling, 'Come over and help us!'

Philippi was the first place in Macedon that Paul and Silas stayed to preach the gospel. In doing so, they took the Good News of Jesus through the open door into Europe. It was a new beginning.

So Paul's encounter with Python occurred at a monumental threshold in faith history: Christianity was in the process of shifting from one continent to another.

Our personal threshold moments may not be as significant as Paul taking the gospel to Europe. But they are still times when God calls us to enter into our calling. Python doesn't attack randomly: it waits for those moments.

Did Python meet its match in Paul? On balance—and I recognise this is an arguable point—my personal opinion is no. Python wasn't overcome by Paul. I lean towards the view that, despite the conversion of the jailer, Paul suffered a significant setback. Python may not have won, but it certainly didn't lose either.

If Paul had stayed in Philippi and followed up the disciples he'd won to Christ, I'd say yes, he definitely overcame Python. If he'd gone on with his ministry in this first town he preached in Macedon, there'd be no question in my mind that he'd whopped this threshold spirit big time. But he left immediately.

Now you may think differently. And I'm open to being persuaded that my view should be modified. However, I believe it's all too easy to think we've overcome Python when outsiders might see our situation another way.

Jentezen Franklin relates a memorable story of how he led his church into overcoming the spirit of Python. The congregation was expanding and a new building was needed to accommodate the growing number of worshippers each week. Just as construction started and all the church's financial reserves had been used to get them to that point, Franklin went to the bank to make a first withdrawal on a secured loan. To his great surprise, given the impeccable credit of the church, the bank's board of directors refused to advance the money or to give an explanation.

'Looking back, I believe with all my heart that this was an attack from our unseen enemy to restrict and coil around our church to stop us from reaching thousands of souls,' Franklin wrote.[12] 'I told the bank president in our meeting that if they didn't keep their word and give us the money as promised for the loan, I would inform our congregation of their actions. He grinned and smugly said, "Do what you like but we will not change our minds."

'That Sunday morning I got up and shared my heavy heart with our congregation. I felt like our vision to reach our city, state, and nation was stopped in its tracks... I shared with the congregation the bad news, then challenged them to do what I was going to do. I had made up my mind to remove my personal bank account from that bank.'...

'The next morning the parking lot of the bank was full. There were nine or ten customers in each line. They were saying, "I'm from Free Chapel and I'm closing my account."

'By noon that day I received a call asking me to attend an emergency meeting the bank had called with its board. When I arrived, they presented a contract for the loan and said, "Preacher, you have just about ruined our bank."'

Franklin, however, inspired by the words of an elderly, trusted minister the night before, rejected the contract and said that he and his church would trust God to provide. And, as he went on to relate, for over a year, financial miracles rained down, perfectly timed to their needs. 'The python's grip on our finances and faith had been broken,' he concluded.

That statement is questionable in my view. Just as it's debatable whether Paul overcame Python at Philippi, I see the situation Franklin describes as decidedly ambivalent.

Franklin rightly discerned that his church was up against Python. As we look closely at his story, there are obvious signs of:

1. surprise strike on a threshold (first withdrawal)
2. most vulnerable moment (all financial reserves used)
3. constriction (no other money)
4. silence (bank board has changed its mind but not said so)
5. intimidation (the ruinous withdrawals)

Now Franklin did not recognise Python as a threshold spirit. Nor apparently did his church realise that Python's pressure is to compel us to sacrifice to it.

In my experience and observation, there are three kinds of sacrifice Python finds acceptable:

1. other people
2. ourselves
3. the honour of God

No doubt many people will see it differently but, as I personally look at Franklin's story, I see two of these three sacrifices being offered to Python. First, there's the bank and the wider community that depends on the bank. This looks remarkably like the sacrifice of others in the name of faith.

As a consequence of this first sacrifice, there's enormous opportunity for this scenario: *'The name of God [to be] blasphemed among the Gentiles because of you.'* (Romans 2:24 NIV)

Perhaps Franklin's church really did overcome Python. I retain a level of doubt, however. Because, if in doing so, they also caused the name of God to be tarnished, then they made a sacrifice of His honour. That then creates the perfect set of circumstances for Leviathan to savage them in the future.

Python has a serpent's subtlety. It can channel us into sacrificing other people's employment, livelihood or future while tempting our hearts to believe that we're actually choosing to exercise faith. *If*, instead of challenging and encouraging his congregation to close their accounts, Franklin had simply chosen to say the church would proceed ahead in faith that God would provide, then the question mark over Python loosening its grip would be resolved.

Ahhh. *If.*

It's always about 'if'.

And it's been that way since the Garden of Eden.

It would be all too easy to get the impression that Python emerges out of nowhere in the Book of Acts, pokes its head up for a brief moment and then promptly gets squashed right back down—never to show its forked, flickering tongue ever again. But that would be a totally inaccurate view. Python was so indecently famous in the ancient world that a writer could easily allude to it without actually naming it.

How did it come by this notoriety?

The fact is Python Apollo had an oracular shrine at Delphi, high on the cliffs above the Bay of Corinth. The resident sibyl—known as the Pythoness or Pythia—was renowned far beyond the borders of Greece. She would sit in a cave on a brass tripod,[13] above a rock crevice from which mind-altering fumes emanated. Speaking sometimes coherently and sometimes in a babble—considered to be an unknown heavenly tongue or a language from the far reaches of the earth—she would make riddling predictions on behalf of the god. The priests apparently charged a fee for interpretation.

For centuries, worshippers and inquirers travelled to Delphi to consult the oracle about the future. Croesus, the king of Lydia in the sixth century before Christ, was famed for his riches. But he was also legendary, long after his time, for sending a messenger to Delphi to seek guidance about going to war with the Persians. Pleased with the oracle's answer, 'If Croesus invades, a great empire will be destroyed,' he failed to notice the ambiguity in the response.

Yes, **ambiguity**. One of the hallmarks of Python.

And *if* as well: 'If Croesus invades...'

Some seven centuries later, the temple at Delphi had grown wealthy and magnificent. Nero visited it and, even before he was made emperor, removed hundreds of its finest marble statues. His acquisition hardly dented its collection. Nero was intrigued by the stylised *E* which was found throughout the temple complex, most notably on the navelstone,[14] which allegedly marked the centre of the world. He asked the priests of Python Apollo to explain the meaning of the *E*.

Plutarch, who later became the high priest there, commented in his essay, *On the E at Delphi*, that in fact no one could be sure. The symbol was so ancient that its true significance was lost in the mists of time.

However, no doubt aware of the unsatisfactory nature of this answer, Plutarch ventured several guesses. It possibly, he said, came from 'ei', meaning *if*. After all, many of the oracle's answers began with *if*. So did many questions put to the Pythoness. Another possibility was that it meant *'I am'* and referred to the god, Python Apollo, himself. Or it might be related to the number *five*.

Now, although Paul—in my view—didn't comprehensively defeat Python at Philippi, he learned from his mistake. And he revealed the secret of overcoming this spirit to the people of Corinth, who lived just across the bay from Delphi.

Although Python isn't specifically mentioned in his letter to them, it's alluded to all the way through chapters 12 and 13 of 1 Corinthians. The original recipients of the letters would have known that all the references to the parts of the body in chapter 12 were harking back to the various votive offerings given to Python in its guise as Asclepius, the god of healing. Our modern medical symbol of the entwined serpents on a staff is that of Asclepius. In Corinth there were famous shrines where gold, silver, pottery and wood body parts, such as arms or legs or torsos or eyes were given as thank-offerings for healing of that afflicted part.

> *Just as a body, though one, has many parts, but all its many parts form one body, so it is with Christ. For we were all baptised by one Spirit so as to form one body—whether Jews or Gentiles, slave or free—and we were all given the one Spirit to drink. Even so the body is not made up of one part but of many. Now if the foot should say, 'Because I am not a hand, I do not belong to the body,' it would not for that reason stop being part of the body. And if the ear should say, 'Because I am not an eye, I do not belong to the body,' it would not for that reason stop being part of the body. If the whole body were an eye, where would the sense of hearing be?*
>
> 1 Corinthians 12:12–17 NIV

Paul is merely stoking the fire at this point, indirectly alluding to the way Asclepius has counterfeited and undermined the Spirit's intention for the church. Asclepius' call to fragmentation worked in the first century and it's still working in the twenty-first. Why change something with such a proven track record? Asclepius prompts many believers to think: 'We don't need to be part of an organised church to worship God,' and even accuse, 'That's the religious spirit in you calling you to institutional settings.'

After the warm-up exercise in chapter 12, Paul turns his attention directly to Python. We call chapter 13 the 'love chapter', but perhaps it's better titled the 'if chapter' or 'choice chapter'.

> ***If*** *I speak in the tongues of men or of angels, but do not have love,* ***I am*** *only a resounding gong or a clanging cymbal.* ***If*** *I have the gift of prophecy and can fathom all mysteries and all knowledge, and* ***if*** *I have a faith that can move mountains, but do not have love,* ***I am*** *nothing.* ***If*** *I give all I possess to the poor and give over my body to hardship that I may boast, but do not have love, I gain nothing.*
>
> 1 Corinthians 13:1–4 NIV

Four uses[15] of 'if' and two of 'I am': both nodding to that famous *E* engraved on the navelstone which Plutarch suggested meant either **if** or **I am**.

But there are further echoes of the rites at Delphi: the tongues of men or angels, the resounding gong, the clanging cymbals, the gift of prophecy, the fathoming of mysteries and revealing of knowledge. All these were features in the temple worship of Python Apollo.

So what, if anything, overcomes the spirit of Python?

Paul tells us of one and only one answer. **Love**.

Perhaps that's why I doubt Jentezen Franklin and his church overcame Python. The reality of everyday life in his congregation may well be different, but the story—at least as he told it—did not exude love at any point.

Faith simply doesn't trump love, even faith that can move mountains.

As soon as we face an 'if' moment, as soon as we're about to step across a threshold where different choices present themselves, Python has a legal right to be there. Where does this right come from?

Let's go back to Genesis chapter 3, verses 13–15. Here it is in the New American Standard Version:

> *The woman said, 'The serpent deceived me, and I ate.'*
>
> *The Lord God said to the serpent, 'Because you have done this, cursed are you… I will put enmity between you and the woman, and between your seed and her seed; he shall bruise you on the head, and you shall bruise him on the heel.'*

That last word, *heel*, is also the Hebrew for *if*. It tells us that God granted to the serpent the right to strike our choices.

This is why ***if*** is so important to Python. This is why it takes **IF** as its symbol. *If* is the word granting it legal entrance into our lives.

If.

If only.

What if.

As I've related different anecdotes throughout this book, you might have wondered if anyone has ever bruised the head of Python while it's been bruising our choices. Yes, Python has indeed met its match. And it met its match in Jesus.

He faced it during the temptation in the wilderness. Look at all the 'ifs' thrown at Him during that time.

> *'If You are the Son of God, tell this stone to become bread.'*
>
> Luke 4:3 NAS

> *'If You are the Son of God, throw Yourself down from here...'*
>
> Luke 4:9 NAS

> *'...if You worship before me, it shall all be Yours.'*
>
> Luke 4:7 NAS

This was a threshold moment in Jesus' life: He was on the verge of public ministry and He was at the end of a forty day fast. Neither Luke in this passage, nor Matthew in chapter 4 of his gospel, identify the spirit he faced. But the evidence is there that the satan, also called 'the tempter' or 'the devil' in this episode, was in fact the spirit of Python. Let's examine the clues:

> *Then the devil took Him to the holy city and set Him on the pinnacle of the temple and said to Him, 'If You are the Son of God, throw yourself down, for it is written, "He will command His angels concerning*

you," and "On their hands they will bear you up, lest you strike your foot against a stone."'

Matthew 4:5–6 ESV

Is this ever a loaded scene!

What is the significance of the devil transporting Jesus to the temple in Jerusalem? Why there? And why that quote? With all of Scripture to choose from, why does the satan pick that particular one?

Two reasons: partly that quote alludes to Python. That's the first reason. But the second is obviously that the satan is dissatisfied with having just a counterfeit navelstone at Delphi. No second-rate copy, thanks. It wants the real deal: and that happens to be the very thing the counterfeit is counterfeiting—the foundation stone of the temple in Jerusalem.[16] This foundation stone is known as the 'eben ha-shetiyah'—*the stone from which the world was woven*.[17] It is the counterpart in the natural world of a spiritual reality: the cornerstone of the created cosmos. The satan, in whisking Jesus off to Jerusalem, had an ambitious masterplan. Just as he'd come to rule the world through tempting the first Adam, he now aspired to the entire universe through tempting the second Adam.

So how does the quote, *'On their hands they will bear you up, lest you strike your foot against a stone,'* allude to Python? It's from Psalm 91 and Jesus would no doubt have mentally gone straight to the next line since, after all, in the first century, the current division into chapters and verses didn't exist. That next line is: *'You will tread on the lion and the adder; the young lion and the serpent you will trample underfoot.'* (Psalm 91:13 ESV)

The Hebrew for adder is 'pethen', *python*.

And in the previous verse, the word for *strike* is 'nagaph', used also for *dash, stumble* and *plague*. It indicates the refusal of a threshold covenant by trampling on a cornerstone and not passing over it. The stone in this verse isn't just any stone—it's a threshold stone. This is about angelic protection to ensure that the cornerstone is not defiled—so that it never becomes a 'miphtan', a threshold defiled by Python. It's about God's assurance He will send His hosts so you don't even accidentally place your foot in such a way that you say 'no' to His covenant.

So, when the satan took Jesus to the top of the temple, that was the background. The tempter was suggesting: 'C'mon Jesus, test it out. God's word says He'll rush angels to ensure Your covenant with Him remains intact.'

Whoa! Look at the gamble on the satan's part. He's raised the stakes by an almost inconceivable degree. And he could not have been certain of the outcome. Or perhaps he thought he could. The Book of Judges is full of classic textbook-style examples of the sad and sorry ends of those who manipulated threshold covenants to their own advantage. And this was what the satan was asking Jesus to do—not to break covenant with God, just to bend it a teeny tiny bit.

What would have happened if Jesus had done exactly as the satan wanted and thrown Himself down from the temple? Well, let's examine the consequences within the possible *ifs* involved here.

Let's suppose that the angels caught Him and held Him up so He alighted ever gently on the ground. Now because this *pass over* of the 'eben ha-shetiyah' was at the satan's instigation, Jesus would have had a threshold covenant with God and also an agreement with the satan. *At one and the same time.* But God has never allowed that sort of unholy compromise at any time in salvation history.

So it's more than likely the angels wouldn't have caught Him as He fell. Whether He killed Himself or not, the satan would have achieved a victory of unimaginable proportions. Because Jesus would have 'dashed His foot against a stone', which means He would have refused to covenant with God—He would have disdained to be one with God. And He would have turned His back on the call on His life.

Moreover, the stone He struck would have been the foundation stone of the temple.

The satan would therefore have triumphed: instead of just ruling this world (John 12:31), he'd be ruling the whole created cosmos.

> *'Submit therefore to God. Resist the devil and he will flee from you.'*
>
> James 4:7 NAS

Resist.

That's what Jesus did when He faced Python.

For many believers, resistance equals knowing Scripture well enough to stand firm in the face of enemy attack. Now, knowing the Bible is fantastic—but it's not enough. In fact, when we're told, as we so often are, just to stand on the Word of God and quote it at the devil so he'll flee, we're being offered the most unholy mixture of truth and lies there could possibly be.

Let's look at the reasons why. When Jesus was atop the temple and the satan was trying to persuade Him to throw Himself over, He answered with this verse: *'Do not put the Lord your God to the test.'* (Matthew 4:7 BSB)

Now Jesus made a choice at that moment. He chose to quote Deuteronomy 6:16. But this is by no means a universal rule. In Malachi 3:10, God invites us to test Him. Moreover, Isaiah rebukes King Ahaz for refusing to put God to the test.

> *'Ask a sign of the Lord your God; let it be deep as Sheol or high as heaven.'*
>
> *But Ahaz said, 'I will not ask, and I will not put the Lord to the test!'*
>
> *Then he* [Isaiah] *said, 'Hear then, O house of David! Is it too little for you to weary men, that you weary my God also? Therefore the Lord Himself will give you a sign...'*
>
> Isaiah 7:11–14 ESV

And, of course, there's Gideon. Now if what Gideon did in asking for various signs and reversed signs involving dew and fleeces wasn't repeatedly putting God to the test, I'm not sure what could ever constitute one.

It's clear there's no total ban on testing God. So, how can anyone know when it's okay to do so and when it's not?

The answer is simple: you ask Him personally. You talk to Him and inquire of Him whether you're in a

Deuteronomy 6:16 situation or a Malachi 3:10 situation. Or something else.

In other words, you foster a relationship with Him. This is the key to the choice Jesus made: His relationship with the Father was such that He knew which alternative to select from amongst a range of Scriptures.

Jesus didn't just rely on His knowledge of Scripture to resist the devil. That's only part of the story. The other part was His relationship with God. His loving, intimate oneness with the Father was what made the devil give up.

Love.

At the end of the day, that's the really simple answer to defeating Python. Jesus modelled it for us but Paul made it explicit when he wrote to the Corinthians.

Love. *'If I speak with the tongues of men or of angels... but have not love... I am nothing...'*

Paul wasn't alone in affirming this solution. The apostle John also told us the answer to overcoming Python was **love**.

In his short first epistle, he uses Python's iconic 'if' 22 times beginning in verse 6 of chapter 1:

> ***If*** *we claim to have fellowship with Him and yet walk in the darkness, we lie and do not live out the truth...*
>
> ***If*** *we claim to be without sin, we deceive ourselves and the truth is not in us.*
>
> ***If*** *we confess our sins, He is faithful and just and will forgive us our sins and purify us from all unrighteousness.*

John doesn't put it quite like this, but we can boil down his words to: if we remain complicit with Python, we're deceiving ourselves if we also think we're under God's protection. If we blame others and refuse to acknowledge that we always have a choice on a threshold, we'll never get out of Python's strangling hold.

Yet if we always choose love, we'll find that there are times when God gives us the sort of miracles that saw Paul and Silas walk out of prison free and clear. When faced with the consequences of opposing Python, Paul didn't moan and say, 'If only I'd left that slave girl alone.' Silas didn't blame Paul: 'If only you'd kept your mouth shut, buddy.'

No, they sang praises to God.

Always a good option, because God comes down to inhabit the praises of His people. (Psalm 22:3) If the key to overcoming Python is love and you're not sure what love looks like in a particular situation, then take a tip from the strategy of Paul and Silas.

Praise God.

And when He arrives to inhabit Your praises, ask Him how best to be the hands and feet of His perfect love.

'When the devil had finished every temptation, he left Him until an opportune time.'

Luke 4:13 BSB

As previously indicated, Python is not only a spirit of thresholds, doorways and beginnings, but also has specific legal rights in those situations. It has God-given permission to strike at our choices—permission given in Eden. Now, since Scripture cannot be broken (John 10:35), this permission is not going to be revoked.

So Python cannot be bound.

Let me repeat that sentence. Python cannot be bound.

God has given us protection against Python but He does not give us permission to bind it.

Jesus didn't try to do so. Neither did Paul.

I believe that Python is a spirit with a similar status to Leviathan, so you might try binding it once but, as Scripture says, you won't attempt it twice (Job 41:8). I take this as a hint: don't even try a first time.

Now sure, Python can be cast out of people, but it cannot be cast out of the situation.

Let me repeat that sentence too. Python can be cast out of people, but it cannot be cast out of the situation.

At Philippi, Paul used his God-given authority, coupled with faith, to cast Python out of a slave girl. However, it's decidedly questionable whether he asked God's permission to do so. *'Paul grew so aggravated that he turned and said to the spirit, "In the name of Jesus Christ I command you to come out of her!"'* (Acts 16:18 BSB) Aggravation is not normally associated with heaven's approval of a request. Now personally I think Paul realised his mistake by the time he got to Corinth—so he looked for a better approach. And while God was able to turn Paul's imprisonment in Philippi to a great good, who knows how many more people in the town would have been saved had Paul and his team not had to leave so abruptly?

Authority simply does not equal permission. Yet we've been trained think it does: that spiritual authority automatically confers divine permission. In fact, it's the other way around. If you seek permission from God and He grants it, you necessarily have any requisite authority. But when you use authority assuming it equals permission, it is far too easy to operate outside God's will.

This question of authority is particularly important when it comes to spirits like Python, Rachab and Leviathan. Python is *not* an ordinary 'daimonion', *demon*, such as those Jesus repeatedly cast out. This cannot be emphasised too strongly. There are cautions throughout the epistles of Jude and Peter about dealing with fallen angelic powers that many believers simply ignore. The spirit of Python is, I believe, one of the 'exousia', *powers*—entities higher in rank than the principalities mentioned by Paul in Ephesians 6:12 and lower in rank than the world-rulers of the same verse.

Python is a spiritual potentate, not a foot-soldier. According to Tom Hawkins, it doesn't appear to desire embodiment in human beings, like 'diamonion' do. However, it may choose to seek embodiment for a particular purpose. When Jesus comes down the Mount of Transfiguration after enacting a threshold covenant for the church, He encountered a boy with a demon. He *rebukes* the demon, it leaves and He tells His bewildered disciples: *'This kind does not go out except by prayer and fasting.'* (Matthew 17:21 NAS)

Here we have Jesus modelling what Jude and Peter encourage us to do: ask the Lord to *rebuke* this threshold guardian. Prayer and fasting make a difference—but even so they must be at the Lord's direction. Relying on a formula or methodology to overcome Python is useless. There are guidelines to follow but, in the end, they are more about what *not* to do, rather than what to do. God has to give you a personal strategy for your unique situation.

The bottom line is: because Python can be cast out of people but not out of the situation, it's going to come back. When it left after tempting Jesus three times, it wasn't forever: it was *'until an opportune time'.*

One of those times was when Jesus went to the Pool of Bethesda where, for 38 years, a man had been waiting for healing. John reports this miracle in the fifth chapter of his gospel. Modern readers generally fail to notice the clues that would have been obvious to John's ancient audience. Using a literary device inspired by Hebrew poetry,[18] John linked this story to Peter's betrayal of Jesus in the house of Caiaphas. Throughout chapter 19 of his gospel, Peter's fall is narrated with repeated allusions, both overt and subtle, to thresholds. The climax of his repeated denial on the threshold is the moment when the cock crows.

A rooster doesn't mean much to most of us. But to the ancients, it wasn't just the herald of dawn—a threshold guardian in the natural world—it was sacred to Asclepius. By linking the story of the healing of the man at the Pool of Bethesda to Peter's betrayal, John left a clue for any astute first-century reader that this wasn't a temple-sanctioned place. It was a shrine to Asclepius.

Present-day archaeology confirms this supposition: this was a colonnade with five porticoes *outside* the walls of Jerusalem, near the Sheep Gate.[19] It seems to have been a shrine to Asclepius. Of course, *inside* the precincts of the sacred city it would be impossible to have a pool dedicated to another god. But *outside* the walls, the Roman occupiers of Judea and other Gentiles could practise their own religion without inciting a riot.

The story itself draws suspicion that the 'angel' who stirred the waters was a fallen entity, not Yahweh's messenger. Would the Healer of Israel have caused strife, hostility and jealousy as those at the pool strove to be the lucky one to get to the water first? Would He have caused such crushing of hope for so many? Would He have promoted manipulation and deceit as the sick scrambled over one another to get to the pool?

No. The Healer I know wants all to be made whole. If He'd sent an angel to stir the waters, then everyone would have been healed, not just one person.

So there is no question in my mind that, when Jesus goes to the Pool of Bethesda, He and Python are in confrontation once more. It's one of those *'opportune times'.* Python is in the guise of Asclepius, the healer.

And what does Jesus do? Quote Scripture, as He did in the wilderness? On the contrary, He seems to ignore Python entirely and focus on the man who was ill.

> *'When Jesus saw him lying there, and knew that he had already been a long time in that condition, He said to him, "Do you wish to get well?" The sick man answered Him, "Sir, I have no man to put me into the pool when the water is stirred up, but while I*

> *am coming, another steps down before me." Jesus said to him, "Get up, pick up your pallet and walk." Immediately the man became well, and picked up his pallet and began to walk.'*
>
> John 5:6–9 NAS

John doesn't mention love here. But in fact, that's what the story's about. The overcoming of Python, without a single nod of acknowledgement in its direction—all through love.

Remember my colleague who went to the theme park and then couldn't make it past the second-last step up to the diving platform?

The classic example of someone who also reached the second-last step but choked on the last is Simon Peter. He made it all the way into the house of Caiaphas but couldn't take the last step of saying he knew Jesus.

The story of the satan sifting him as wheat is given in John 18. This story is packed full of words that, in the first century, a Greek or Hebrew reader would have immediately recognised as alluding to thresholds. Many minor details, not strictly necessary for the storyline, seem to be included for the specific purpose of emphasising that this is the moment when Simon Peter is summoned into his calling and steps up to the threshold—only to get comprehensively pulverised by Python.

These details include the repeated mention of the doorkeeper as he is initially barred at the door. Another is one of the attendants to the high priest slapping Jesus with the palm of his hand. In all the indignities offered to our Saviour, why is this comparatively trivial one mentioned? I believe it's to emphasise that this passage is threshold-related: one word for *cornerstone*—that is, the *threshold stone*—is derived from the word for the *palm of the hand*. So is the name *Caiaphas*. So is *Cephas*, the Hebrew cognate of the name Peter.

At the threshold into our true calling, a sacrifice must be made. Because of fear, one of the choices we often make at the threshold is to offer up the honour of God as our sacrifice. This is what Simon Peter did as he stood at the fire. He dishonoured Jesus by refusing to acknowledge Him as his rabbi.

It was at another fire, on another threshold, a few weeks later that Peter was given the opportunity to re-affirm that honour. And guess what? Yes, the conversation is all about the only way to overcome Python: **love**.

> *When they had finished breakfast, Jesus said to Simon Peter, 'Simon, son of John, do you love Me more than these?'*
>
> *He said to Him, 'Yes, Lord; You know that I love You.'*
>
> *He said to him, 'Feed My lambs.' He said to him a second time, 'Simon, son of John, do you love Me?'*
>
> *He said to Him, 'Yes, Lord; You know that I love You.'*
>
> *He said to him, 'Tend My sheep.' He said to him the third time, 'Simon, son of John, do you love Me?'*
>
> *Peter was grieved because He said to him the third time, 'Do you love Me?' and he said to Him, 'Lord, you know everything; You know that I love You.'*

Jesus said to him, 'Feed My sheep.'

John 21:15–17 ESV

The nuances of this conversation don't come out well in English. Jesus asks Peter if he loves Him sacrificially (with agápē) and Peter responds with honesty that his love is at the level of friendship (with phileo). Jesus asks again and Peter repeats his answer. So Jesus, on the third time, asks Peter if he loves Him as a friend.

Isn't it so reassuring that Jesus meets us where we are and is willing to take us by the hand and carry us over the threshold?

Threshold: the last step, the first rung, the final day, the introduction, the open door into a new beginning, the end of an era, the beginning of another, a boundary, a frontier, a limit.

Whatever a threshold looks like, it doesn't take a degree in rocket science to identify the symptoms of a threshold covenant along with the activity of Python.

Two brothers from Syria, along with their wives and children, had been waiting almost fifteen years to immigrate to the United States. Refugees from the civil war, as well as orthodox Christians who had been promised priority status as a persecuted minority, they had fled through Lebanon with just sixteen suitcases. Their relatives in America, Sarmad and Sarah Assali, ensured that their green cards and visas had been approved and a house was waiting for them on arrival.

They had reached the final step—the families had left Beirut on a flight to Qatar en route to America. While they were in the air, President Trump signed an executive order limiting entry to the US by Syrian citizens. Blocked at the airport, they were not permitted to contact their relatives. So, stymied by their limited English and the silence regarding their rights, they were obliged to take the next flight back.

The **constriction** is evident, so is the **silence**. There is wasting as well (although this is not strictly—at least so I believe—the activity of Python, but rather of its ally, Rachab). Implied in the encounter with immigration officials is **intimidation** and pressure to make the **sacrifice** and back away from the threshold.

There are countless stories, many far more tragic. The young girl involved in a fatal accident on a sideshow ride her first day out of training at an amusement park. The man who, with his son, was disabled in a car accident on his way to pick up first prize in an international novel-writing contest. The rising athletic star who was king-hit by a drunk on New Year's Day and suffered brain damage. The man who, having worked for fifteen years through the intricacies of estate law to distribute an inheritance according to his friend's wishes and who was within hours of winding it all up, received an unexpected message from a solicitor wanting to question the provisions of the will.

Every week I hear anecdotes about people on the verge of a new beginning or a significant breakthrough who are caught, suddenly and unexpectedly, in the coils of Python. Sometimes I'm even part of other people's stories. Because I've been involved in writing groups, both Christian and secular, for nearly forty years, I've witnessed countless people self-sabotage on the threshold of publication. They don't listen. They think God's call will protect them.

Yet, from simple things like spelling errors in the first sentence (no surer way to get a manuscript instantly rejected—editors can't possibly read through the thousands of manuscripts in the slush pile each year and often discard a book in the opening line) to not checking the contract (surely a publishing house specialising in Christian books would be ethically above reproach!) to paying tens of thousands for a book to be published (when it will only ever recoup thousands), the marks of Python are everywhere.

A friend of mine heard me asking about constriction and wasting: I was posing questions to ascertain just how many believers are affected by Python. At first—rather naïvely—I thought it was rare. During the writing of *God's Pageantry*, I was even under the impression that Jentezen Franklin and his church had overcome Python, but that he didn't really understand what it meant to be in its clutches for decades. I surmised that, because of his generational lineage, things went well for him. Nevertheless, my lingering doubt about the effect on the bank and the wider community did cause me to continue to delve into Python's strategies. During this period, my friend said, 'I don't believe any of this. I preach and teach on this. It's simply not true. If you know your authority, and are exercising it within your God-given jurisdiction, spirits like Python and Leviathan are as dust beneath your feet.'

Then she decided to write a book. It took a while but eventually she said, 'You could be right about Python, after all. I have never experienced anything like what's happening. I also have realised I've never before said, "This is my calling." I feel God wants me to do this book and it's like nothing I've felt about anything else previously.'

How do you know if you are afflicted by Python? Well, hopefully by now, the stories throughout this book have given you a good feel for what the issues are.

Let me reiterate. The most obvious symptom of an attack by Python is: you experience severe **constriction** whenever you try to come into the calling God has placed on your life. As you try to cross the threshold into your destiny, you're squeezed in any or all of the following: finances, time, resources, personnel, relationships, personal circumstances, health, physical capability, appearance, social networks, educational qualifications, requisite documentation, information.

Everything in your personal world is squashed, choked, pressured, crushed, tightened, quashed.

In effect, the choices of your past and the 'ifs' of the moment have caught up with you.

Prayer

I re-affirm my commitment to You—Yahweh Nissi, the Lord my Banner, the Lord my Bridegroom, the Lord my covenant defender, the Lord my Miracle-giver. I acknowledge Jesus as my personal Saviour; and I renounce and revoke any covenant I have with Python because of ancestral trading or because of my own sacrifices on the threshold.

When I was complicit with Python, I dishonoured You. Forgive me. When I offered up others as a sacrifice, denying them advancement into their calling, I dishonoured them and also myself. Forgive me. When I denied my own integrity, I denied Your truth and sacrificed my own honour. Forgive me.

Forgive me for the many ways, known and unknown, I have sided with Python against You. Forgive me for the times I've forgotten that it is not my faith that will carry me over the threshold, but only the faith of Jesus as I hold onto the hem of His garment.

Abba Father, keep me mindful that the battle is already won and that Jesus has already made the required sacrifice for the threshold into my calling. Remind me when Python assails me to say, 'The Lord rebuke you, Python. Jesus is my all-sufficient sacrifice. No other is needed. And if you think differently, take it up with Him.'

Thank you, Abba, for casting out my fear with Your love and reminding me that, like Jesus, I can tackle powerful cosmic entities through Your grace and holding on to His hand.

I ask You, Yahweh Nissi, for the love, the grace, the wisdom and the courage to accomplish all that you have assigned me to do. Teach me what love looks like in each situation and, when I am tempted to use my own unredeemed, unregenerate love instead of Your agápē, nail it to the Cross of Jesus. Thank You that His Blood makes it possible to overcome Python through love.

Thank you for Your blessing. Keep me close to Your heart. In the name of Jesus, the One who stands at the door and knocks. Amen.

4

Python and Yoga

Arpana Dev Sangamithra

YOGA. THE VERY WORD BRINGS to mind thoughts of peace... or pain, depending on your experience. Excellent exercise. Great to tone the body. Smiley, shiny people who sometimes use mysterious words like 'the universe' and 'being centred' and so on. Sometimes they rave on about organic, vegan, cosmic, moon and a bunch of other new-age trendy-type terms. Most people love yoga!

And then there are people like me. I wanted to like yoga... but I just couldn't. For years, a strange feeling rose inside of me and I wanted to be anywhere other than near a yoga place. My friends practised—to great benefit. One of them is actually a successful teacher now. I couldn't understand this hesitation—or maybe I didn't want to define it.

There is some comfort in not knowing. I avoid knowing until it hurts. Then, I have to give in and sit down and have a chat with Abba.

And so, after a while, as I do with everything in my life, I took the matter up to God. I asked Him, 'What's the deal with yoga? And what's the deal with Christian yoga? Is there such a thing? Can it just be an exercise, if instead of chanting *om*, I chant *Jesus*?'

I didn't get any direct answers. Instead, it was a series of revelations over a few months... and it continues. Of late, I've been in more than one conversation with fellow Christians who have similar questions about yoga. So, let me share what I've learned.

I've organised the main points in as simple a way a possible, with relevant information. There is a lot to summarise, so please try to see the connections between certain words and concepts as you go along.

I can speak with a certain amount of authority on this topic—I am Christian, I am Indian, I was a Hindu, I was a Bharatanatyam dancer for over ten years. Half my family is still Hindu. This knowledge is part of my ministry and calling.

1. Yoga is, without any shadow of doubt, a Hindu religious practice. The origins are supposedly very ancient. Some people suggest as long ago as five thousand years. That, if true, would put it back before the time of Abraham. However, there is a universal acknowledgment that the poses, as currently practised, are much more modern. Possibly just a couple of hundred years old.

2. The root word for *yoga* is the Sanskrit word 'yuj', literally meaning *to yoke, to bind*. The wider sense is *to yoke to a spirit*. Sometimes it is meant as *a union, to discipline, to subjugate* in the sense of *subjugating the body and mind*. Indeed, *subjugate* itself means *to bring under the yoke*. Now it's not just the Sanskrit *yoga* with a root of 'yuj'. The root of the English word

yoke is also 'yuj'. Hence, the meaning of both *yoke* and *yoga* are interconnected.

On a spiritual level, the discipline of yoga and its offer of peace stands in direct contrast to the comfort and rest offered by Jesus: *'Come to Me, all who are weary and heavy-laden, and I will give you rest. Take My yoke upon you and learn from Me, for I am gentle and humble in heart, and you will find rest for your souls. For My yoke is easy and My burden is light.'* (Matthew 11:28–30 NAS)

3. Yoga is mentioned in ancient Hindu texts like the *Rig-veda*. It is also mentioned in the *Bhagvad gita*, one of the most revered of Hindu texts. Yoga is fundamentally religious in nature; it is in essence a spiritual discipline, not a method of physical exercise.

4. The study of yoga is called the *yoga-sutra*. The word 'sutra' means *thread*. The etymology of this word derives from a language even more ancient that Sanskrit: the Pali tongue. This is not only the original language of the subcontinent of India but also that of Buddhism. The root words, 'syū' and 'sū' are connected with *binding* or *sewing*, and go back to *thread* and *needle*—those items which sew and hold things together. Contextually, *sutra* is a text of rules, a manual. (Remember 'kama-sutra'? It is a manual for 'kama' or *sexual desire*.) Those root elements, 'syū' and 'sū', are also the basis of the English word, 'suture', *the surgical stitching of a wound*.

It's also hypothesised that 'syū' and 'sū' are, in some mysterious fashion, the root of the word *hymn*.[20] If true, this would suggest that a hymn binds us to God—and perhaps there's more than a sprinkling of truth in that idea since, as Psalm 22:3 tells us, God inhabits the praises of His people.

5. In context, the word *bind* in relation to yoga-sutra is to be understood as referring to an individual who is trying to concentrate with complete and undiverted attention. The purpose of such unqualified focus is to channel their awareness to a higher being. In other words, *meditation*. Okay, you may think. Sounds good. The Bible commands us to meditate on the promises of God, on His saving acts of long ago, on His holy Word. Not so good! Biblical meditation is entirely different from meditation in yoga, Hinduism or Buddhism.

   Binding has almost the same nuances in the Hebrew Scriptures as it does in the discipline of yoga. In both cases, it's about binding ourselves to a spirit. The difference is, of course, which spirit we bind ourselves to.

   'Wait for the Lord; be strong and let your heart take courage; wait for the Lord!' says Psalm 27:14 ESV. The word 'qavah', which is rendered *wait* in the vast majority of English versions, also means *bind*. So this could be: *'Bind yourself to the Lord; be strong and let your heart take courage; bind yourself to the Lord!'* [21]

6. One significant aspect of yoga is the idea of the *chakra*. A chakra is simply a wheel, but contextually, the seven (yes, seven!) chakras are supposed to be the seven main nodes of energy in a person. There are several other chakras and some of them are hidden. Each chakra represents a different energy. Western philosophers took this understanding and reinterpreted it to match both medicine and

temperaments and pretty much reorganised the idea to make it more acceptable. People like Carl Jung used it to explain the personality and develop psychological theories while others, like Deepak Chopra, made it still more popular.

7. The energy from these nodes supposedly flows through the body via the nerves. So, the nervous system is involved.

8. Each chakra has a religious Hindu significance. It is possible to trace almost every aspect of these wheels back to the spiritual realm. These wheels of the spirit, of course, point to the description of the cherubim as in the vision of Ezekiel as he speaks of them in chapter 10 and 11 of his prophecy. And don't forget that Python is a fallen cherub—still counterfeiting the ways of God and the designs of heaven.

9. The one at the very top of the head, the *'crown chakra'*, is associated with the brain and the nervous system, as well as cognition and consciousness. This chakra is supposed to be the one that contains wisdom and the ability to connect with the 'formless, limitless, higher consciousness, ecstasy, bliss and divinity'. In Hinduism and Buddhism, this is within every person, the self. This is the origin of the phrase 'becoming one with the self'.

10. The chakra in the pelvis area, somewhere near the coccyx, is called the *'mooladhara chakra'.* 'Mooladhara' means *the very root, the fundamental, the foundation of identity*. It is a combination of two words—'moola' (*the first, foundational*) and 'adhara' (*identity*). This foundational chakra is related to

instinct and survival. I don't typically quote wiki, but it is the most comprehensive description I've seen so far. Wikipedia says that: physically, mooladhara governs sexuality, mentally it governs stability, emotionally it governs sensuality, and spiritually it governs a sense of security. This is where the *'kundalini'* lies dormant.

11. Kundalini is the most primal 'shakti' (that is, *energy* or *strength*). Kundalini is the unconscious, sexual, instinctive force and is said to be connected to the mother goddess or mother energy, 'aadi parashakti' (that is, *the first* or *the all-encompassing energy.*) Kundalini is represented as a sleeping serpent ('-lini' from 'linde', *snake*) that lies coiled at the base of the spine.

12. The kundalini serpent—yes, Python by any other name—is coiled three times around the 'swayambu lingam'. 'Swayambu' means *self-manifested.* 'Lingam' simply is a *penis*. It is a phallic symbol. Worshipped by devotees, it is used to represent the Hindu god known as Shiva—a deity who is both a benefactor and a destroyer. In fact, *the* destroyer.

13. Awakening the kundalini serpent, which is wrapped three times around this self-manifested phallic symbol, allegedly leads to deep meditation, enlightenment and bliss. When the kundalini is awakened, and/or invoked, the kundalini energy is said to travel through the nerves and the rest of the chakras to connect to the crown chakra and eventually to the 'supreme being'—in this case, Shiva.

14. Shiva is one of the holy trinity of Hinduism. This guy is an ascetic, and sits meditating for the most part. His image is adorned with snakes—kundalini serpents. The main one is a black cobra. This is wrapped around his neck three times and also around the linga or the penis. The penis here is represented as a stump or stone on the ground—no images of the male anatomy are ever used. Small mercy, I guess!

15. The kundalini is invoked or awakened by the practice of kundalinin yoga and the more popular hatha yoga. Hatha has several meanings and it is interpreted in many ways. One of the meanings of 'hatha', pronounced haTa is *stubborness*, or *willfulness*.

16. 'Om' is the most sacred sound and mantra or chant in Hinduism, Buddhism, Jainism and Sikhism. It is said that, when chanted, it is at the same frequency as everything in nature. This breath exercise is more than it seems on the surface. If we examine the word *breath* in the Scripture, *'Then the Lord God formed a man... and breathed into his nostrils the **breath** of life, and the man became a living soul,'* we discover that God gives life through naming. The use of 'om' as a breathing exercise is about displacing the name of God in a person's life for that of another god.

17. Yoga postures are not innocent. The first of them after the usual chanting of 'om'—an invocation of the 'higher consciousness' (not the creator God who has revealed Himself in Jesus)—is the 'surya namaskara' or the *sun salutation*. Through this posture, your whole mind, body and soul is saluting a sun god. As simple as that. No amount of chanting Jesus is

going to change the fact that you are worshipping the sun with your body. (And, no surprise here, as we zip over to the Mediterranean for a moment, that Python is linked with Apollo, one of the sun gods of both the Greek and Roman pantheons.)

18. The lotus position is another classic example of distortion, which involves kundalini. The pose seems as simple as 'criss-cross apple sauce'—also called the 'tailor position' or 'Indian style'—and yet... it opens up your pelvis. It is a deeply sexual position. Depending on the 'mudra' or *hand gesture* used, you either connect to the supreme conscious through your crown chakra or else invite the supreme conscious for a sexual intercourse via the spiritual realm. This is where the third eye chakra is activated. Again, the connection goes right back to Shiva because he has a third eye on his forehead.

19. 'Shavasana' or the *corpse* pose is one where you lie as still as a *dead body* or 'shava'. It is a way to invoke death. And on and on... each position in yoga has a much deeper meaning that meets the eye.

20. Lastly, I'd like to mention 'namaste'. Translated, it means: *I recognise the divine in you and bow to it.*

The Bible is very clear. Romans 12:1–2 NIV says:

'Therefore, I urge you, brothers and sisters, in view of God's mercy, to offer your bodies as a living sacrifice, holy and pleasing to God—this is your true and proper worship. Do not conform to the pattern of this world, but be transformed by the renewing of your mind. Then you will be able to test and approve what God's will is—His good, pleasing and perfect will.'

We are to keep our bodies pure and holy. Simple as that!

In summary: yoga is not—in any way, shape or form—devoid of harm. Almost all the poses in yoga, as well as Indian classical dance, are designed to open your mind and body to the spirit realm. The same applies for reiki and all the new age alternative therapies... including Tibetan crystal bowls. I know from experience... I used to be an Indian classical dancer.

Open-mindedness needs to be one-directional: we need to be open to the Holy Spirit more than the world around us. He *will* tell us when we are not doing something safe or sensible. And at that time, we'd better listen, even if His instruction is not pleasing to us.

One of the key differentiators between Christianity and other religions is the surrendering of your 'self' to Christ. It is *not* emptying of the mind, rather allowing the Holy Spirit to lead you in all walks of life.

Yes, God has given us a free will but it is wrong to say He approves of everything we do with that free will. We must test everything against Scripture. Nowhere in the Bible is it written that God approves of us opening ourselves to other spirits and energies. Neither is it Scriptural to want a separation between the Church and what we do in our lives. His words are eternal and unchangeable. And He is immutable!

I understand that many people are seeking God. But, to find God, people have to first let go of every false idea they already have about God. He created the universe, but the universe is not God. There is a huge difference between worshipping the Creator and worshipping what He created.

God is love and He personified it for the propitiation of all mankind. But He is also an all-consuming Fire... He has never tolerated dilution or adulteration of the message of Christ crucified with other religions. If you think that God... the one true God, is okay with overlapping religious theories, you are mistaken.

Hosea 4:6 NAS offers us a warning that we do well to meditate upon:

> *'My people are destroyed for lack of knowledge. Because you have rejected knowledge, I also will reject you from being My priest. Since you have forgotten the law of your God, I also will forget your children.'*

But the remedy is already at hand. Jesus of Nazareth—the Lord Himself.

Shalom, shalom!

Prayer

Yahweh Rapha, You are the Great Physician and Healer. I come before You and I confess I have not looked to You as my first refuge. I repent of failing to seek You as my hiding place. Please forgive me.

You have made provision for healing in so many ways: by Your sovereign intervention; by medical and scientific knowledge given to health professionals and practitioners; by the wondrous ability of the body to heal itself. Yet, behind all these is Jesus lifted up to heal all our diseases, in the same way as Moses lifted up the bronze serpent in the wilderness. It is truly through the power of the Cross of Jesus and His stripes that we are restored.

Forgive me, Lord, for the times I have forgotten this. Forgive me too for the times I've turned Your best gifts into idols, just as the bronze snake became an idol. I have sought Your gifts, not You as the Giver. I have sought provision, not You as the Provider. I have sought healing, not You as the Healer.

Forgive me for all the times I've hastened first to other modes of health and wellbeing and forgotten You. I repent of all beliefs and activities that have made an idol of Your gifts to me. Keep me ever-mindful that You and You alone are the Giver of life and wellbeing, appropriate exercise regimes and breathing arts, the skills of medical practitioners, the beneficial properties of vitamins, minerals, supplements, herbs, oils and foods.

Smash any idol in my life and direct me back to You as the Giver of all wonderful gifts to sustain and nurture me—physically, emotionally, mentally and spiritually.

This I ask in the name of Jesus of Nazareth, our Saviour, Healer and Lord. Amen.

5

Python Goes Down for the Count

The serpent is the most obvious symbol of Python. When God sends us dreams to tip us off about an imminent attack or an ongoing siege by this spirit, it commonly appears as some kind of serpent. It can be a cobra or an adder, an asp, a viper or a boa constrictor but the message is basically the same. God is alerting us in a way that is relatively easy to interpret that we're about to face the spirit of Python.

However, a serpent is not the only warning symbol He can send our way. Cultural and national nuances can play their part. For instance, there are no snakes in New Zealand. The Māori word, 'whēke', to squeeze or crush, is related to 'wheke', octopus. So, if you're a Kiwi, an octopus can substitute as a symbol of Python.

Many Australians, both indigenous and non-indigenous, are apt to relate the Rainbow Serpent to Python, but my personal view is that—generally speaking—it's more closely connected with the fallen seraph, Leviathan. Similarly, in China, the widespread dragon motif seems more of a Leviathan image than one of Python. This is an important distinction because these two spirits hold entirely different offices in the spirit realm. Thus, entirely different strategies are needed to dismiss them.

Other symbols of Python include: the staff of the medical profession—with its entwined serpents of Asclepius; the rooster; the letter *E*; the word *if*; the bruised or bitten heel; yoga and its associated kundalini; as well as the various iconic movie characters I've already mentioned such as Darth Vader.

In addition, a doorway or an entrance—particularly one with a sense of menace about it—is indicative of the presence of a threshold guardian. The sentinel at the gate may not be Python, the spirit of constriction; it may instead be Rachab, the spirit of wasting. They're allies in this business of keeping us from fulfilling our destiny.

In addition, there are numbers Python wants to claim.

Python has laid claim to the iconic word IF as its symbol. It's also put in its stake for a couple of specific numbers: 5 and 101. In ancient Greece, numbers were not simply abstract concepts used for calculation; they had profound religious overtones. The holiest number was ten when it was arranged like this:

This is the tetract—or tetrakys—the number 10 in a triangular array.[22] Pythagoras, the mathematician who made your life difficult in high school with his theorem about the square on the hypotenuse, held this arrangement to be a transcendent reality. 'All is number' or 'God is number' was the dictum of the Brotherhood he founded. Nonetheless there were 'good' numbers and 'evil' numbers, including one that was considered such an 'atrocity' it was avoided at all costs. On the other hand, the ten of the tetrakys was worshipped as Manifest Deity, the source of nature, the Number of Numbers, the Meaning of Meaning, the creative principle, the fundamental Truth of the universe, the heart of the Logos.

John, when he opened his gospel with a proclamation of the Logos, took on Python by taking on Pythagoreanism. He made absolutely sure that anyone reading it who was influenced by this religion, either through Platonism or Gnosticism, didn't mistake Jesus for the tetrakys. He did this by simply making his opening sentence 17 words long. His use of 17 might result for us in a shrug and a 'so what?' of complete indifference, but any first century Greek reader knew that 17 was the 'atrocity' to be avoided at all costs. In the philosophy of truth and beauty that dominated Greek art, architecture and literature, 17 was the 'antiphraxis', the *obstruction* that was viewed by the Pythagoreans with loathing.[23] To the Greek readers of John's gospel, his opening line would have been an iconoclastic explosion: to unite the despised 17 with the exquisitely beautiful number, the 'logos', was unthinkable.

Are you thinking: 'What? The *logos* is a number?' Yes, it means both *word* and *ratio*. When the term, 'THE logos', was used it referred to the mathematical concept we call the golden ratio. And it's not inappropriate that John should have used this double meaning because the golden ratio is the divine mathematical signature found in all created things. It is also found throughout the first chapter of Genesis and, in particular, in Genesis 1:1 alone, it can be found three times in the underlying mathematical structure.

What does that mean: the 'underlying mathematical structure'?

It's important to understand that in classical Greece as well as in ancient Israel, there were no separate figures for numbers as we have today. Letters did double duty as both the building blocks of words and of numbers. Thus, every Bible verse—simply because each letter is also a number—has an underlying mathematical design.

It might seem that modern mathematics, by taking on the figure shapes of the Hindu-Arabic system, got rid of its religious baggage. It divorced itself from the Greek notion of numbers as divine which came from the Pythagoreans, as well as from the kabbalistic mysticism that grew up in Hebrew circles. But that would not be the case. The Hindu-Arabic system also emerged from a religious philosophy—one so opposed to Christianity that its introduction during the medieval period was vehemently opposed in Europe.

The notion of 'zero' did not exist in the West until the coming of the Hindu-Arabic system. The idea was rooted in the Hindu-Buddhist concept of nirvana. It was seen as a diabolic concept by many people during the Middle Ages—in many ways, they could foresee the societal change its widespread acceptance would bring. The pressure to adopt it came through trade. But the wise could see the end result: once you can say that certain objects were worth nothing, it was just a small step to applying that to people. From there, it's another small step to things—and people—being worth less than nothing.

Life might have been stratified by class in the Middle Ages, but everyone was worth *something*. As a result of losing the battle against the introduction of zero, a cultural chasm of mind-blowing proportions exists between our present age and medieval times. We are on the far side of a philosophic divide where it is possible, as a society, to view other people, as well as ourselves, as being worth *nothing* or *less than nothing*.

But back to Python and the Brotherhood indirectly named for it: the Pythagoreans. They might disdain 17, but on the other hand, 5 and 101 were mouth-watering prospects.

The number 5 was chosen simply because in the Greek way of writing it was epsilon, *E*, already claimed by Python Apollo because it was engraved on the navelstone at Delphi.

101 is more complex to explain. Not much is actually known about the life of Pythagoras. Some eight hundred years after he died, a catechism for the Pythagorean religion, which fused mathematics and magic, was written by Iamblichus. *On the Pythagorean Life* was a Q&A of doctrine made famous by Julian, the nephew of Emperor Constantine. Julian turned his back on Christianity and, on coming to the throne, decided to overturn his uncle's decrees. However, his view was that Constantine had done little more than accede to the will of the people in legalising Christianity—and removing it was going to take far more than an imperial decree. He sent to the shrine of Python Apollo at Delphi for

advice and, in addition, promoted various works about Pythagoreanism as the basis of an ethical alternative to Christianity.

The last oracle of the Pythia was sent back to Julian:

> *'Tell to the king that the cavern wall is fallen in decay;*
> *Apollo has no chapel left, no prophesying bay,*
> *No talking stream. The stream is dry that had so much to say.'*

In the catechism, *On the Pythagorean Life*, was this sequence:

> Question: What is the oracle of Delphi?
> Answer: The tetraktys. It is also the harmony in which the Sirens sing.

Iamblichus was both revealing and concealing in this statement. The tetraktys—or tetract—was those ten dots arranged in a triangle which was the ultimate mystical symbol of the Pythagoreans. As mentioned just a few pages back, it was regarded as Manifest Deity, the source of nature, the Number of Numbers, the Meaning of Meaning, the creative principle, the fundamental Truth of the universe, the heart of the Logos.

And by Logos, they didn't mean Jesus of Nazareth. (There were some exceptions—some Gnostics appear to have considered Jesus to be the re-incarnation of Pythagoras.)

However, by saying the oracle of Delphi is the tetraktys, Iamblichus was asserting that it is the true god. Hidden in this enigmatic answer is a claim that Pythagoras (either as Python Apollo or perhaps Hyperborean Apollo) is the creator of the cosmos. In addition, the remark about the Sirens is not any old throwaway line. The Sirens were supposed to sing one note each of the Pythagorean musical scale and thereby sustain the universe through the Music of the Spheres.

Now, there are parts of this philosophy not far from Judeo-Christian belief. The Hebrews believed that God created the universe through words. Basically, the alphabet was the essence behind creation. But since letters were also numbers, then particular equations were the motive power of creation.

Stephen Hawking in *A Brief History of Time* pondered the fact that there is no particular reason our system of science and mathematics should actually work in any practical, predictive sense. 'What is it,' he asked, 'that breathes fire into the equations and makes a universe for them to describe?'

The divide between science and religion today reflects the ancient partition between the adherents of Pythagoreanism and Christianity. Python Apollo, said the Pythagorean catechism, is the creator and sustainer of the universe. Not so, said the Christians. The true answer would be Jesus.

Music sustained the universe, said the Pythagoreans. And there's a little known fact about stringed musical instruments that they considered religiously significant. It's almost universally said that, if one string is double the length of another, they will be an octave apart. That's a generalisation that's not quite accurate. Creating a perfect octave on a stringed instrument is not actually a matter of doubling the length of the string. There is a tiny difference in size, equivalent to just over 101%. Today this is called a 'Pythagorean comma' or 'diatonic comma'.

101 is a number Python would like for its own. Because if it could convince us that it is and we started agreeing with it, then we'd basically be saying God isn't the sustainer of the universe.

Too many believers already implicitly deny that God is the Creator of the cosmos by declaring that the pentagram belongs to the satan or to practitioners of witchcraft or dismissing it as a new age obsession.

Who made the pentagram? Who graced the cross-sections of apples, pears and pawpaws, the shape of starfish and the imprinted design on sand dollars, the petalled stars of windflowers and borage, buttercups, primroses, geraniums, pansies and flower varieties beyond number with the basic shape of a pentagram? The satan? Or God?

The basic mathematics of a pentagram, the golden ratio, undergirds Genesis 1:1. To say therefore that a pentagram is satanic in origin is to buy into a lie. In effect—although this is surely never the intention of believers who make such statements—it's to deny that the Logos is the Creator.

Similarly, the mathematics of 101 undergirds Paul's epistle to the Ephesians. Straight after the opening salutation comes Ephesians 1:3–14, which in Greek is a mammoth, intricate 202–word sentence. Almost at the very end of the epistle is Ephesians 6:12–18 which describes the armour of God in 101 words.[24]

That 202-word sentence is dominated by ideas about God sustaining the Christian. The armour of God is about God protecting the Christian community. And one of the specific features of that protective armour is its ability to ward off Python.

We can be sure of this because the Greek word, 'belos', which is translated *darts* or *arrows* fired by the evil one, is also the word for *threshold*. And not just any threshold: a defiled one. One that a thief has broken into. It's an almost perfect equivalent for 'miphtan', the Hebrew word to describe a *threshold violated by Python*.

The initiation rite into the Masonic Lodge invokes Python in several different ways. The candidate is dressed in pyjamas, with a blindfold over his eyes and a noose around his neck. His left trouser leg is rolled up and he wears one slipper and one shoe, or else one slipper while his other foot is bare. His left breast is also bared, then pricked with a dagger or compass.

This introduction to the Lodge is primarily about **intimidation**—a tactic of Python. It's also of course about **silence** as to what is about to transpire. There are many **ambiguous** and liminal aspects to the ceremony. The symbolism of being on a boundary/threshold is evident: the candidate is neither fully clothed nor naked, he is neither bound nor unbound, neither free nor a slave, neither seeing nor sightless, neither barefoot nor shod.

The removal of the shoe is said to have Biblical origins. When Boaz becomes the kinsman-redeemer of Ruth, he is given another's sandal to indicate his new responsibilities and the passing over of inheritance rights. However, this may be far from the only reason. A shoe was removed and the foot placed inside the skin of an animal as part of the *hemingr* rite of adoption amongst the Vikings.[25] In both the case of Boaz and the Norse adoption rite, the issue is two-fold—matters of inheritance and of being brought within the fold of a family. In the cultures of the Far East, the removal of shoes for slippers is indicative of crossing a threshold: outside footwear must be replaced by what is appropriate for inside. This may be bare feet or slippers. The space inside a home, like that inside God's temple, is a 'covenantal space'.

Such a distinction is made within Paul's description of the Armour of God.

> *'As shoes for your feet... put on the readiness given by the gospel of peace.'*
>
> Ephesians 6:15 ESV

Despite the impression given by many English translations, there is no word for *shoes* in the Greek. The word 'hupodeó' is *underbinding* for the feet. Paul had many options from sandals to military boots, but he chose something that is more like our modern socks than anything else. Once we realise that the Armour of God is given to us, as a corporate church, to cross thresholds, we see the sense of this.

When Joshua crossed the threshold into the Promised Land and ratified the covenant with God through circumcision, he met with the Commander of the Armies of the Lord.

> *'Take off your sandals,' says the Commander, 'for the place where you are standing is holy.'*
>
> Joshua 5:15 NIV

Just so, beyond the threshold inside the Inner Court of the Temple, the Levites go barefoot. Paul's description of the armour that God gives us for warfare doesn't make sense unless we realise it is also priestly garb.

The *noose*, or *cabletow*, which is part of the Masonic initiation rite, is the clearest evidence in the whole ceremony of Python's part in it.

The sons of Anak who so terrified ten of the twelve spies sent to reconnoitre the Promised Land were Ahiman, Sheshai and Talmai. These giant descendants of the Nephilim acted just like threshold guardians. As the twelve spies scouted into Hebron, they encountered these massive watchmen and they panicked.

Let's look at the names in this last paragraph more closely: at the gateway to the Promised Land, as they entered Hebron, *the passage*, they met the sons of Anak, *the choker*, whose names were Talmai, *the one who causes doubt*, Ahiman, *my brother is like me*, and Sheshai, *alabaster (floor)*.[26] While I have translated Anak above as *choker*, it is sometimes rendered *necklace*.[27] But because it goes back to *strangle*, it therefore seems to me very likely that '*necklace*' is a sanitised rendering of *noose*.

The reality is that Python and its gargantuan back-up bullies are not specific to the Masonic Lodge. We face them every time we approach our own personal 'Promised Land': the destiny to which God calls us. As we come to the gateway, we encounter the spiritual equivalents of Talmai, Ahiman and Sheshai.

Most of us, unfortunately, have tried to buy them off instead of asking the Holy Spirit how to deal with them.

Worse, we don't learn from our mistakes. When circumstances are against us; when we're ruinously cheated of the money we want to invest in furthering our dreams; when we wind up paying a debt we don't owe; when we don't have time to give to our calling; when our hard work is stolen by another person who claims it as his own; when the promotion we should have received is given to someone with less experience and fewer qualifications and we are asked to mentor them—we try another carefully crafted solution of our own instead of asking God what the real problem is!

When you feel, as one of my friends put it, even before knowing anything about thresholds, 'like a boa constrictor's got hold of my life', you start by going to God as your refuge.

And that means giving up your habitual ways of comfort and consolation in times of trouble. You can't effectively break off a covenant with Python until you've turned aside from your false refuges and sought the face of God.

Intimacy with God. Loving God with all our hearts, minds, soul and strength. We are so scared of the thought. Utterly terrified by it.

We have more in common with the elders invited up the mountain to a banquet with God who came down the mountain and participated in the sin of the golden calf than we care to admit.[28] That's why Python has such a hold on us. We're more frightened of getting close to God than we are of tangling with the constrictor. We're like moths, dazzled by the flame of His love, but tortured by the possibility we'll be consumed in His fire.

For some of us—men, in particular—this fear of intimacy shows up in a dislike of modern worship songs with their emphasis on the heart. We'd far rather the traditional hymns with their solid theology and emphasis on the mind. The truth is we're called to love God with *both* heart and mind.

And love sometimes involves apologising. Some of us, however, find it almost impossible to say 'sorry' to God. And we even develop theologies that suggest we don't need to confess and repent, because 'it's all done at the Cross'. That cliché enables us to ignore Scriptures like:

> ***If** we say we have no sin, we deceive ourselves, and the truth is not in us. **If** we confess our sins, he is faithful and just to forgive us our sins and to cleanse us from all unrighteousness.*
>
> 1 John 1:8–9 ESV

> *...**if** you have committed any sins, you will be forgiven. Confess your sins to each other and pray for each other so that you may be healed.*
>
> James 5:15–16 NLT

Sometimes we manipulate God-given blessings to avoid saying 'sorry' and being restored to Him. One of the more recent ways of doing this is to declare Python to be bound or pronounce a death sentence on Leviathan or decree that Rachab is forbidden to test us. We want a 'powerful, effective' prayer or a prophetic word that's going to make a dramatic, instant change.

Sometimes we stand more emphatically on the Word of God, exercising faith more loudly and more fervently.

We visualise the promises of God coming to pass in our situation. Such attitudes come perilously close to magical thinking—and even practice.

When I was a teenager, I developed a habit of spinning in a circle. Every time I felt anxious or distressed, I would simply get up and twirl around like a spinning top until I felt better. I stopped this practice decades ago—largely because I came to live in smaller houses without the space required.

I didn't even remember this habit until I came to research threshold covenants. I had struck a problem with my investigations: Google, in tracking my browsing history, was busy refining my search results into ever narrower categories. So, to 'trick' it, I'd occasionally throw in a completely random term. One particular day, my totally impulsive combination was 'threshold' and 'Turkish Delight'. I was stunned to see millions of new options open up. And all of them seemed to be about whirling dervishes—the Sufi dancers who wear a white robe, a black cloak and a brown cap and who spin around in a circle.

'Dervish' means *threshold*.

As soon as I saw the meaning, my mind pulled up the memory file of my teenage years and all those times I'd spun in a circle whenever I felt troubled or upset. I knew instantly it was a false refuge: it was a source of comfort that substituted for God as my tower, refuge and strength in times of trouble.

With a dizzying feeling of horror, I went to God and asked Him what He thought about it. He left me in no doubt. For the next two weeks, I felt as if I was in a tar pit—that spinning I'd indulged in was far from innocent. As I looked deeper into the meaning of the dervish and its threshold connotations, I became more aware of why God considered my actions unwholesome. I was trying to leap over my own shadow—an impossible feat that can only be achieved by operating in the supernatural. I couldn't even begin to imagine why I was trying to do this.

So I asked God. And His simple answer was that, even as a teenager, I was instinctively aware of the perils of the threshold, and sensing Python and its allies, I was trying to use magic to avoid them. I was trying to use a 'counterfeit' threshold to ward off the dangers of the real one. The whirling of the dervishes mimics the whirling wheels of the cherubim,

I had some big-time repentance to do.

But the experience of those two weeks in the tar pit left an indelible mark on me: when believers tell me they've never had anything to do with magic, I reserve judgment. All they are really saying is that they've never *knowingly* had anything to do with magic.

Yet the modern church is deeply infiltrated with the practice of magic. There are so many subtle ways it can insinuate itself into our thinking. We can, for instance, take one verse and use it as a talisman, ignoring its context or any conditions that might be attached to it. The verse becomes the promise we cling to.

Sometimes this is fine but—when we cling to a promise and not to God, we have the relationship inverted.

When we decree or declare in a way that violates Scripture, we have crossed a line into the practice of magic. It's low level but it's not without consequences. Because we are using our own power of delivering a prophetic word to stand against God's word, we are attempting to countermand His decrees with our own.

When we go into the court of heaven to receive a judgment in our favour, we are approaching the Lord, the Judge of all the earth. All too often we're too busy to take the time to ask our advocate, the Holy Spirit, the best approach for us. Instead we use other people's legal procedures and protocols because those ways worked for them.

God will sometimes answer our prayers miraculously. He'll occasionally render an instant verdict in our favour. But His main criteria is that it brings us closer to Him. If answering our prayer will just solve our problems so we can continue without Him, it's not going to happen.

Relationship.
Trust.
Intimacy.
Fidelity.
Love.

They all begin with turning your back on your false refuges, saying a sincere 'sorry' and turning back to Him.

This is a trustworthy saying:
If *we died with Him,*
we will also live with Him;
If *we endure,*
we will also reign with Him;

If we deny Him,
He will also deny us;
If we are faithless,
He remains faithful,
for He cannot deny Himself.

2 Timothy 2:11-13 BSB

This passage is, at one and the same time, both reassuring and disturbing. The mysterious occurrence of four *'ifs'* suggests it's about Python. Why four? Honestly, I have no idea. However four 'ifs' appear in the 'choice chapter', 1 Corinthians 13, as well as Philippians 2:1. Perhaps 'four' is some subtle allusion to the four faces of the cherubim—lion, eagle, ox, human—or the four compass points or the four seasons.

What is the difference between being faithless to Jesus and denying Him? This is a question I've wrestled with and I have no sure answer. Ultimately, I think only God can judge our hearts in this regard. But as I've watched people try to come into their calling and begin a shuffle with Python, I have a few thoughts.

First, Jeremiah was right when he said, *'The heart is deceitful above all things, and desperately wicked: who can know it?'* (Jeremiah 17:9 KJV) Who, indeed? When God doesn't deliver on His promise to our timetable, what prompts so many people today to try to help Him out? And help Him in ways that are explicitly forbidden in Scripture?

Believers are not only dabbling in necromancy, but asking others for prayer cover for their activities. The 'Christian version' of necromancy is going to the grave of a renowned minister, seeking his mantle. Believers are not only dabbling in clairvoyance, but defiling others with their divinations. The 'Christian version' of clairvoyance is seen as an aspect of prophecy, but it's a counterfeit. Believers are not only entering temples and shrines to curse the gods there, they are encouraging others to come with them. This 'Christian version' of spiritual warfare brings with it 'the error of Balaam', the enticement to come out from under God's protection by stepping over a threshold and thereby making a covenant with the very gods they've come to curse.

All this showy, dramatic stuff simply avoids repentance. Instead of dealing with hidden sin, instead of turning around and renouncing our complicity with the iniquities of our ancestors, instead of dealing with our own snarled nest of sinful responses and unholy attitudes, we try to find an easy way to cross the threshold. A proven formula to deal with Python. An inside track to make it into our calling.

But God doesn't want to have a second-hand relationship; He doesn't want us to be a friend of a friend. He wants to *know* us, and us to *know* Him. That's *know* as in *covenantal intimacy*.

God wants us to deal with the selfish motivations—the tangle of ambition, pride, desire for money or fame—we have for crossing the threshold. He wants us to deal with our false refuges—the comforts and consolations we have apart from Him. And He wants us to deal with the fear that pushes us back from the threshold too. He knows we don't fully trust Him. If we did, we'd have made it over the threshold long ago.

He wants us to deal with the disease of modern Christianity—the celebration of independence and rugged individuality. The desire to separate ourselves from the Body of Christ and the justifications for confessing only to God, not to one another. No wonder there is little healing. James tells us to pray for each other and confess to each other, *so that* we may be healed. The reality is, if we're praying only to God and our hearts are in denial, then Python is able to obscure what needs to really be confessed. We need trusted people who can take us through a process of sanctification and teach us the laws of the spiritual harvest, so that we can understand how we got to be in the mess we're in.

The first law of the spiritual harvest is: *we reap what we sow*. Many people think this doesn't apply post-Resurrection. However, it is Paul post-Resurrection who says, *'Do not be deceived, God is not mocked; for whatever a man sows, this he will also reap.'* (Galatians 6:7 NAS)

Jesus reframes this principle so that we can avoid its negative aspects. *'Do to others as you would have them do to you.'* (Matthew 7:12 BSB) This golden rule is the touchstone of practical love.

In the spiritual warfare of the last few decades, these principles have been largely ignored. If, for example, you ascend by faith to the third heaven in order to 'bomb' the second heaven where the satan, the prince of the power of the air, has his seat, what does the law of sowing and reaping tell you? It tells you you'll get 'bombed' back. If, for another example, you keep cursing the satan or even addressing him in anger to tell him he's a loser, what does the law of sowing and reaping tell you?

Where are there prayers addressed to the satan anywhere in Scripture? Occasionally I have had a spirit abuse me verbally. My response is always the same:

'Take it up with the Lord Jesus Christ.' There's no reason to dialogue with the powers of darkness.

And there's a very good reason why Paul eventually discovered love is the answer. The law of sowing and reaping tells us that, if we sow love, that's what we'll get back.

When I go to God to ask Him for a strategy regarding an angelic potentate, I think carefully about His answer. It's got to be something that I'd feel comfortable in having done back to me! As you begin to recognise the schemes of the enemy, it's wise to be in constant communication with God. The satan will know that you know his game plan and will try to counteract that. He will try to find unrepented sin, iniquity and transgressions from your past—legal grounds for attack—in order to inflict as much damage as possible as his time grows short.

The more you clean yourself up spiritually, the more you'll need to continue to clean yourself up spiritually. This isn't about salvation but sanctification. And if you don't know where to begin, ask the Holy Spirit to help you find a healing ministry somewhere near you.

In modern Christianity, we shy away from Jesus' message of the narrow gate. Immediately before it—perhaps not surprisingly—He articulates the golden rule, with its subtle message that we should sow well in order to reap well. And immediately after it, He talks about knowing people by the 'fruit' they produce. That 'fruit' metaphor is again about the law of sowing and reaping.

> *...whatever you want people to do for you, do the same for them, because this summarises the Law and the Prophets. Go in through the narrow gate,*

because the gate is wide and the road is spacious that leads to destruction, and many people are entering by it. How narrow is the gate and how constricted is the road that leads to life, and there aren't many people who find it! Beware of false prophets who come to you in sheep's clothing but inwardly are savage wolves. You will know them by their fruit. Grapes aren't gathered from thorns, or figs from thistles, are they? In the same way, every good tree produces good fruit, but a rotten tree produces bad fruit. A good tree cannot produce bad fruit, and a rotten tree cannot produce good fruit... So by their fruit you will know them. Not everyone who keeps saying to me, "Lord, Lord," will get into the kingdom from heaven, but only the person who keeps doing the will of my Father in heaven.'

Matthew 7:12-21 ISV

In Luke 13:22-27, Jesus makes similar statements linking the narrow door to knowing Him. Not saying, 'Lord, Lord,' but actually knowing Him and being covenantally intimate with Him. Showing the 'fruit' that honours Him.

We need to subject ourselves to the Gardener's pruning. Because when we're operating out of a defiled idea of love, honour and trust, or a tainted image of the Father Heart of God, it's only going to play into the enemy's hands.

If love overcomes Python, then we need to know what love is. We not only need to get rid of our false refuges but also our false notions of love.

I was at a seminar when the speaker said that the opposite of love was fear. He backed up this statement with: *'...perfect love casts out fear...'* (1 John 4:18 NAS) I'd always thought the opposite of love was indifference, so his comment was thought-provoking. I wasn't willing to buy into it immediately, but I was open to the possibility he might be right.

As the seminar continued, I started to understand his position. He spoke of the difficulties of convincing his board to back his God-given vision; his frustrations with their timidity, caution and lack of courage. He spoke of all he'd overcome in the past and saw it as a blueprint for the future. As a child, he'd had a rare medical condition and an extremely short life expectancy. His parents had taken him overseas for radical surgery in the hopes of a cure. The first six patients who had undergone this surgery had died. He was the seventh—the miracle child who'd survived and thrived.

Suddenly I understood. This man's definition of love was high-level risk.

His parents had borrowed all they could to take him overseas for an immensely risky operation with potentially fatal consequences. That was his model of what love looked like.

So when his board expressed caution about the costs of implementing his vision, he not only saw them as fearful and cowardly, but as lacking in love. Because they weren't risk-takers, he railed at them for not being loving.

All of us have our own identifications of love. And when other people fail to fulfil our very specialised criteria, we write them off as unloving, uncharitable, unkind.

Unredeemed, unregenerate love is as toxic as true love is restorative.

John Sandford maintains that even the good within us has to be taken to the Cross and offered up. (Prayer ministries specialising in processes of sanctification are, by the way, good places to start the journey of return to God.)[29] We must allow Jesus to slay our natural love and to resurrect it as supernatural love. All the defilements accompanying our private notions of what love looks like have to be cleansed through His blood so we can participate in God's embrace for us and the world.

'What does love look like in this situation?' is the question we need to ask as we approach a threshold and front up to Python.

If we love God, we will not sacrifice His name or His honour.

If we love our neighbours, colleagues, partners, friends and family, we will not sacrifice them on the threshold.

If we love ourselves, we won't sacrifice us either.

We will instead admit that Jesus is the all-sufficient sacrifice and His love has paid the price. That admission must be more than head-knowledge. It must be imprinted in our hearts so deeply that we go to Him and ask Him what He thinks love looks like in these circumstances. Our desire must be to honour that sacrifice He made for us. Yes, it comes back—once again—to talking with Him. To deepening the relationship. To intimacy.

The very thing we so desperately want to avoid.

There are certain times when Python, for all its legal and legalistic delight in *IF*, wants to remove our knowledge of its very existence.

Such a time is when we are confronted by a Scripture like this:

> *'**If** we confess our sins, He is faithful and righteous to forgive us our sins and cleanse us from all unrighteousness.'*
>
> 1 John 1:9 NAS

Many people read this as: *'He is faithful and righteous to forgive us our sins and cleanse us from all unrighteousness.'* By removing all aspect of confession, we delete the very thing designed to bring us closer to God.

Or another:

> *'This is the confidence which we have before Him, that, **if** we ask anything according to His will, He hears us.'*
>
> 1 John 5:14 NAS

'But of course we are asking according to His will!' say so many believers. 'We have the mind of Christ!'

Here's another:

> *'Do not be deceived, God is not mocked; for whatever a man sows, this he will also reap... Let us not lose heart in doing good, for in due time we will reap **if** we do not grow weary.'*
>
> Galatians 6:7;9 NAS

Which so often gets truncated to: *'Whatever a man sows, this he will also reap... Let us not lose heart in doing good, for in due time we will reap.'* Let's accentuate the positive and remove all the negative connotations and the conditional clauses. So many people tell me that the Cross of Jesus has done away with all this negative reaping and that it only happens when our old mindset holds sway and we give room to the negative in our lives. Now, where exactly does Paul say that the Cross of Christ combined with positive thinking will overturn what he wrote here to the believers in Galatia?

The Cross of Christ is about salvation. Don't confuse that with sanctification.

Python can't influence our salvation in any way. Neither can we, for that matter. We can't add anything to what Jesus did on the Cross, we can't subtract anything from it. It's perfectly finished—a done deal.

Confession simply means *agreeing with God.* That's why there's confession of sin and also confession of faith. We can agree with God that we've transgressed against Him but we can also agree with Him about who He is and what He's like.

When we confess sin, we agree with God and break agreement with Python. If we take steps towards severing our covenant with the guardians of the threshold, God will forgive:

> *'The prayer offered in faith will restore the one who is sick... and **if** he has committed sins, they will be forgiven him. Therefore, confess your sins to one another, and pray for one another so that you may be healed.'*
>
> James 5:15–16 NAS

The usual makeover of this verse removes the confession of sin. *'The prayer offered in faith will restore the one who is sick... Therefore... pray for one another so that you may be healed.'* So many of us want to believe we don't have anything to confess because we're innocent.

We're never innocent. We might be made righteous through the power of the blood of Jesus but that doesn't make us innocent.

The human heart tends to fall for one of two temptations: to always blame others or always blame ourselves. We make ourselves into gods or worms.

Python doesn't mind which we choose. It doesn't care whether we sacrifice ourselves or others. But the last thing it wants is for us to turn to God, ask Him what love looks like and then make the choice to implement His answer.

> *'Love is patient, love is kind. It does not envy, it does not boast, it is not proud.'*

1 Corinthians 13:4 BSB

It does not boast, it is not proud: this is a barely veiled allusion to Python's allies—Rachab the arrogant, and Leviathan, the king of the sons of pride.

It does not envy: here's a reference to Python's parting trick. The Greek legend of the defeat of Python includes it rotting away. The Greek 'phtheírō', *decay, breakdown, corrupt* was understood to derive via 'phthónos', *envy,* from pytho, *Python*. It is used throughout the New Testament to refer to *moral corruption.* We can be tempted even as Python leaves—in fact, we can be tempted by its exit to exult and boast of our victory. We thereby draw to ourselves Rachab, the waster and the one who puffs up.

If we stay close to Jesus, He can make a way where there is no way. But if we don't, we can fall even in the moment of victory.

Jesus Himself talks about the spirits behind envy—from His day to ours called the 'Evil Eye' in many places throughout the world. The connecting paragraph between two thoughts on the use and misuse of money is a direct reference to this spirit.

> *'Do not store up for yourselves treasures on earth, where moth and rust destroy, and where thieves break in and steal. But store up for yourselves treasures in heaven, where neither moth nor rust destroys, and where thieves do not break in or steal; for where your treasure is, there your heart will be also.*
>
> *The eye is the lamp of the body; so then if your eye is clear, your whole body will be full of light. But if your eye is bad, your whole body will be full of darkness. If then the light that is in you is darkness, how great is the darkness!*
>
> *No one can serve two masters; for either he will hate the one and love the other, or he will be devoted to one and despise the other. You cannot serve God and wealth [mammon].'*
>
> Matthew 6:19–24 NAS

Here the translation says, 'if your eye is bad,' contrasting it with the clear eye ('phōteinos', *full of light*.) However, the actual Greek word for *bad* is 'poneros', *evil*. Jesus is talking about jealousy of the possessions of others which brings us into agreement with a spirit of hoarding, wealth accumulation and amassing of treasure that has no alignment with the purposes and heart of God.

Jealousy is anti-love.[30] It brings us into accord with Python, even as it is defeated. It robs us of light. We cannot serve both God and money, or God and Python either.

I love this particular gospel passage. Not for anything to do with Python but because it brings to the forefront Jesus the literary artist, the masterful poet, the punster par excellence. Kenneth Bailey points out that the parallel passage in Luke, if translated back into Aramaic, is a masterwork of stunning verse in the Hebrew style.[31]

God is a poet.[32] Jesus, of course, therefore has to be. But it's not just Aramaic verse here. It's multilingual! Jesus used Greek as well to implicitly contrast the poetic assonances, 'phthónos', *envy*, and 'phōteinos', *full of light*.

What's He telling us here? He's telling us that our complicity with Python amounts to hatred of God. We might sacrifice others, or self-sabotage and sacrifice ourselves, or alternatively pay Python's fee with the honour of God—all of them choices to serve a master other than Abba Father. We've walked away from love. Often while deluding ourselves we've done exactly the opposite.

What does love look like? What—actually—is love?

Paul talked a lot about love to the Corinthians, subtly alluding to Python as he did so, but he didn't answer the question of what it is.

To do that, let's turn to another threshold moment in Scripture. One we examined briefly before: the incident in the Valley of Acacias, when the people of Israel were on the verge of the entry to the Promised Land. There Python, in the guise of Baal Peor, *lord of the opening*, trotted out the ploy of seduction.

Balaam the diviner from Pethor had, after having failed three times to curse the Israelites at the behest of the king of Moab, got his pay by devising a plan to get the Israelites to curse themselves. Balaam realised God was never going to break covenant with His people, so he came up with a strategy to tempt the Israelites to break covenant with Him. Through eating food sacrificed to Baal Peor and through ritual prostitution—sexual union to 'become one with the god Peor'—some of the people, including some clan princes, covenanted with Python.

God therefore withdrew His own covenantal protection and over twenty thousand people died from plague.

Moses and the elders were at the entrance to the Tabernacle weeping and repenting before God when Zimri, a prince of the tribe of Simeon, went past, flaunting an illicit relationship with Cozbi, a Midianite princess.

Phinehas, the grandson of Aaron, grabbed a spear and went after them. He killed them both, the plague stopped, and God commended him. Phinehas was rewarded with an everlasting priesthood and a covenant of peace.

I'm not going to quote from Scripture because, as I've said in *God's Priority,* I believe all current English translations, while not actually wrong, are deficient. They say that Phinehas went after Zimri and Cozbi into the 'qubbah', *tent*. In other instances, 'qubbah' is translated *curse*.

I believe 'curse' is the correct translation. Phinehas voluntarily entered the curse, taking upon himself the potential consequences of his action. Like Jesus, he was willing to suffer death to bring healing to the people. And like Jesus, he was given a covenant of peace and an everlasting priesthood.

What does love look like? It looks like a willingness to enter the curse... with no guarantee of the outcome. That's what love of God and neighbour looks like. When we stand in harm's way on behalf of others, we risk our own lives.

Python, in its guise as Baal Peor, turns up in John's vision in the Book of Revelation. We can be sure of this by the reference to Balaam's teaching. Note the similarity of 'Peor' to the first syllable of the name of the church in this passage:

> *'Write this letter to the angel of the church in Pergamum. This is the message from the one with the sharp two-edged sword: "I know that you live in the city where Satan has his throne, yet you have remained loyal to me. You refused to deny me even when Antipas, my faithful witness, was martyred among you there in Satan's city. But I have a few complaints against you. You tolerate some among you whose teaching is like that of Balaam, who showed Balak how to trip up the people of Israel. He taught them to sin by eating food offered to idols and by committing sexual sin. In a similar way, you have some Nicolaitans among you who follow the same teaching. Repent of your sin, or I will come to*

you suddenly and fight against them with the sword of my mouth. Anyone with ears to hear must listen to the Spirit and understand what he is saying to the churches. To everyone who is victorious I will give some of the manna that has been hidden away in heaven. And I will give to each one a white stone, and on the stone will be engraved a new name that no one understands except the one who receives it.'

Revelation 2:12-17 NLT

In the late nineteenth century, German archaeologists unearthed the temple of Zeus at Pergamum—it is its central monumental altar that is believed to be what John called *'the seat of Satan'*. They took the temple apart stone by stone, shipped it back to Berlin and displayed it in its own museum. In the 1930s, Albert Speer re-created this edifice as a backdrop for the Nuremberg rallies at Zeppelintribüne, placing a podium for Hitler where the altar would have been.

Hitler traded on the spiritual power of this seat of Satan, this throne of Baal Peor. And when we agree with Python, we are no better. Like Esau trading his birthright for some 'red',[33] we exchange our inheritance for a worthless lie.

The defilement from the altar of Pergamum, according to John's account in Revelation, comes from tolerating the teaching of Balaam. That is, the seductive error that we can indulge in sin and still enjoy the favour of God. Throughout modern Christianity, this is the clarion call: you don't have to obey God to enjoy His favour. You just have to subscribe to the right set of beliefs. (Yeah, I know—wrong! We're saved by grace through faith. So why do so many of us act as if we're saved by doctrine?

Why do so many believers 'unfriend' others for having a 'religious spirit'? Why do so many people sever fellowship with others because they don't believe the 'right thing'? Don't mistake me. Doctrine is important. Very important. But it isn't going to save anyone. Knowing the right things about God is not the same as *knowing* God in covenant.)

The enticement of Baal Peor, the god who guarded the threshold to the Promised Land, is epitomised by the modern misunderstanding of grace. Baal Peor's stronghold lay above the Valley of Acacias—the place where the city of Sodom had been. The long shadow of Sodom is found in the widespread current belief that grace means it doesn't really matter about my relationship with God. He loves me unconditionally.

Many decades ago, I went to a Christian camp and there I saw a graphic illustration of the theological concept of substitutionary atonement. The teacher had three wooden crosses on a board. They symbolised Jesus and the two thieves—one who was crucified on His right and one on His left. The crosses which depicted the two thieves had black bags hooked over them to represent sin. The central cross, because Jesus was sinless, had no bag on it.

The teacher explained how the thief who acknowledged his sin and asked Jesus to remember him when He came into His kingdom effectively handed over his black bundle to Jesus. He moved the little bag from the thief's cross to the central one to show that the weight of all his sin and the punishment he was due to reap was transferred to Jesus.

Now, I don't know about anyone else watching but

my appalled reaction was: 'No! Is this what it means to acknowledge and confess sin? I never realised this was what it was about. No way. I am not having Jesus suffering even the tiniest bit more on my behalf. No. No. No. Not one second longer.' Instead of praying as the leader suggested, I turned angrily on God. 'You've heard my last confession.'

I doubt if there has ever been a time in my life when I have been more acutely aware of my own sinfulness than in the months that followed. At the end of each day, I would take mental stock and announce, 'Today I committed these sins. And I am not confessing any of them. I do not want Jesus to suffer any more pain. Am I making myself perfectly clear?' Then, ironically, I would give Him a list of the very things I was telling Him I was not confessing.

After a few months, I had got into a habit of driving home from work and sitting in my car for a while as I '*not* confessed' to God. One day, even before I opened the conversation, I sensed His incredible sadness. 'What's wrong?' I asked Him.

'You,' He said. 'Why won't you accept the fact that this was a done deal nearly two thousand years ago? That you can't change it. It's history.'

I was so upset. 'That's not fair! I don't want to hurt Jesus. But I don't want You to be so sad, either.' I sighed. 'Oh, all right, I give in. But I don't have to like this, do I?'

'What makes you think I do?'

As I look back on this conversation, I see in my theological struggle the issues surrounding grace that everyone faces at the threshold. Maybe not explicitly, but implicitly. Crossing a threshold into your calling not only means that God becomes your covenant defender, it also means that you become friends.

The mark of friendship is not loyalty to one another—though that, of course, is part of it. It's the sharing of secrets. That sharing of secrets first happens straight after Abraham and God complete a threshold covenant. The secret is about the fate of Sodom and Gomorrah.

So, to complete your calling, you have to step into the place where you become a 'friend of God'. And here's the paradox: to do that, you have to accept the fact that Jesus is the all-sufficient sacrifice for your sin.

Think about it. Here's the process: admit that you murdered Jesus—and that He paid the penalty for that murder on your behalf—then turn around and ask Him to be your friend.

Oh, God help us if we don't feel the horror of this. The surpassing grace that God offers us. The unbelievable, lavish forgiveness that He extends to us while holding out His hand to invite us over the threshold.

God wants to covenant with us. But we want to trade. And in wanting to trade, we are vastly more open to Python's offer than God's. God wants to redeem what Python has defiled but, for so many of us, the price of His friendship is too high. Because He will point out areas in our life needing change. He'll ask us to repent; to confess—*agree with Him*—about what needs cleansing in our life.

And He won't set to work until we give Him permission.

As we look back on the times we've faced Python, it's a good thing to identify our weak spots when it comes to temptation and testing. Where in the process we become unstuck.

> **Constriction.**
> **Silence and ambiguity.**
> **Divination.**
> **Intimidation.**
> **Seduction.**
> **Illness and torment.**

In the past, it hasn't taken me long at all. I come undone at **silence**. Oftentimes, I've failed to realise it's even there. But when I have recognised it's there, I've tried to break it and, when that's failed, to simply outwait it. 'Wait on the Lord,' I've said to myself.

But I now realise my error. Waiting, while doing nothing, was just simply putting myself into the hands of Python's ally—Rachab, the spirit of wasting, whom Isaiah calls the 'do-nothing'.[34]

'Waiting' on the Lord is not really *waiting*. At least it shouldn't be.

In Hebrew, *wait* has the sense of *bind*. 'Wait on the Lord' really means *bind yourself to Him*.

I've always loved the Irish loricas. Particularly *The Deer's Cry* which also goes by the name *St Patrick's Breastplate*.

> *I bind unto myself today*
> *the strong name of the Trinity*
> *by invocation of the same,*
> *the Three in One and One in Three.*

I bind this day to me forever,
by power of faith, Christ's incarnation,
his baptism in the Jordan river,
his death on cross for my salvation,
his bursting from the spiced tomb,
his riding up the heavenly way,
his coming at the day of doom,
I bind unto myself today.

Christ be with me, Christ within me,
Christ behind me, Christ before me,
Christ beside me, Christ to win me,
Christ to comfort and restore me.
Christ beneath me, Christ above me,
Christ in quiet, Christ in danger,
Christ in hearts of all that love me,
Christ in mouth of friend and stranger.

The loricas belong to the 'psalms and hymns and spiritual songs' that Paul directs us to use as music in our heart. They are about protection; they are a form of prayer and, as such, form part of the armour of God. Paul learned that lesson in prison in Philippi.

The armour of God is specifically designed for crossing thresholds. It's perfect against Python. I'm not going to go into detail about the armour because I've discussed it at length in *God's Pageantry* and *God's Pottery*. If you want to know more about the music, the mathematics, the gemstones, the flowers, the parts of a doorway, the kiss of heaven and earth, the geography, the priestly garments and the opposition to Ephesian Artemis encoded in that passage, then check out those books.

God wants to put armour on us. And He wants us to put armour on others.

How do we do that? The simplest way is to ask for His kiss. For ourselves and for others.

In Hebrew, the word for *to kiss* is the same as *to put on armour*. And Paul has encoded the elements of the kiss of heaven and earth from Psalm 85:10–11 in his description of the Armour of God.

Yes, we're back to intimacy with God. That's our surest defence against the wiles of Python.

Not only can we ask God for a kiss but, once we've got rid of our false refuge—and that takes not just repentance but testing—we can ask for a change in the guard over the threshold into our calling.

The ceremonial trooping of the colours in Britain takes about forty-five minutes. The changing of the guard in the Vatican is less formal and takes only about a minute. But it takes God about half that to 'change the guard' watching over the threshold of your life—if you ask Him and if you've renounced your false refuges first.

Notice the ***if**s.

Half minute in heaven's time is several months in earthly time (2 Peter 3:8)—and this seems like forever to the children of the 21st century who want what we want this instant.

If the conditions are fulfilled—that is, you've renounced your false refuges and you have been tested to see if you still run to them in times of trouble, then you can ask God to dismiss the old ungodly watchers and replace them with His loyal angelic cohort. You can ask Him to do more than rebuke Python, you can ask Him to seat guardian angels where Python and Rachab have been.

Make no mistake: this changing of the spiritual guard over the threshold into your calling is, in many ways, just as ceremonious as any earthly custom.

First and foremost, you should ask God to grant His permission for the change. Permission works both ways. We have to grant Him permission to come into the specific areas of our lives that He spotlights, while He has to grant us permission in specific areas as well.

The pre-requisite to that permission is always the same: we forgive, we repent, we revoke, we renounce, we repudiate our false refuge and we ask God to raze it. Forgiveness does not mean excusing, rationalising or exonerating. It means speaking words of pardon and asking Jesus to empower those words. Repent means choosing to turn around and change our behaviour. Renouncing means saying an eternal no to past ways of thinking. Asking God to raze our false refuge doesn't necessarily mean we never do that activity again but that we don't use it as a way of avoiding God.

Then we allow Him to rebuke any ungodly spirits (and this might involve repenting of going beyond our own jurisdiction in the past with regard to these spirits.)

God has to grant His permission before we can ask for a change in the guard. Why is this? Because what we're asking Him to do is put holy cherubim on our threshold.

And know what? They'll be looking for righteousness. Or what can be credited as righteousness: faith.

We have no more chance of passing them than we do of passing Python. What will they accept that makes the situation different? They accept the commands of God. They will look at you, shake their fourfold heads, then look at your engraved invitation to come into a threshold covenant with God. They will no doubt wonder why He wants to you to be called 'Friend of God' but they recognise the blood of Jesus in the signature on the invitation. And they will let you pass.

How long does it take for the holy cherubim to replace Python and its crew?

Not long in heavenly time. But it's a different matter in terrestrial time.

So you wait.

You 'wait on the Lord': you bind yourself to Him.

Our wrestling is not against flesh and blood, but against the principalities, against the powers, against the world's rulers of the darkness of this age, and against the spiritual hosts of wickedness in the heavenly places.

Ephesians 6:12 HNV

It's my belief that Python and its allies belong to a class of angelic being called the 'exousias', translated *powers above*.[35] These entities are, in my understanding, a higher rank than *principalities* and a lower one than *world-rulers*.[36] Some of these *powers* belong to the cherubim—others do not. The spirit of Leviathan, for instance, is clearly a fallen seraph.

Although Python, because of its fallen nature, would be naturally hostile to the likes of Leviathan, nevertheless they put aside any infighting in a common cause. They conspire together to stop the likes of you and me crossing the threshold into our calling. Any enmity they feel for one another—and there is plenty—is swept away to make sure we never reach our destiny. They will never stop opposing us, never cease in their efforts to ensure that we never cross the boundary from 'child of God' to 'friend of God'.

They can't afford to. Because ultimately—not immediately, but ultimately—if they don't stop us, they will die. That's the end prophesied in Psalm 82: they are immortal beings who will die like mortal men for their perpetuation of injustice and malice towards us.

Once, however, we do cross that threshold, God immediately bestows on us an honour we can hardly begin to comprehend. As friends of God, we are also invited to the council of God. Just as friends share secrets, so we begin to be entrusted with private confidences from God. Like Abraham when he received a threshold covenant and became the 'Friend of God', through those secrets, we are given the privilege of negotiating with God Himself regarding the fate of cities and nations.

When God takes you into His confidence about a coming judgment, He's coming as a just Judge asking you to give Him a reason to be merciful. When God told Abraham the secret that He had come as a Judge in the matter of Sodom and Gomorrah, He allowed Abraham to appeal the sentence.

It's as if Abraham became not just a 'Friend of God' but a 'Friend of the Court'.

In Australia, a Friend of the Court is an unpaid position that is never advertised. It is the sole prerogative of the judge to appoint a Friend of the Court in any particular case. The appointee must receive no benefit from the position, must take no side in a case and must be completely independent and impartial. There is a similar system in the United States called 'amicus curiae'.

The judicial system can be mechanical, formulaic and legalistic, with an emphasis on a lawyer's ability to make a case. Vital evidence may be suppressed because of a technicality or simple ignorance. Mercy for the accused or justice for the victim can easily be trampled on during court proceedings. The law may be upheld but justice denied. In addition, unnecessary burdens may be placed on society.

A Friend of the Court keeps the overall situation in mind and aims to uphold all the court should stand for: uncompromised truth, promotion of peace, justice for the victim, both mercy and justice for the accused, minimisation of costs and burdens to society—preferably, in fact, an outcome that benefits all of society. If a Friend of the Court can negotiate for a judgment that pleases every party—prosecution, defence and the judge—then it's a win all around.

This is not dissimilar to our post-threshold calling within the Council of God. We can't ask for anything: for example, we can't ask for world peace because God's Word says there will always be wars and rumours of wars. But we can ask for the minimisation of war.

We can't ask for God's judgments to be overturned. Because we'd be asking Him to negate His righteousness, holiness and justice. But we can ask for minimisation of what we are due to reap—and thus for mercy.

> [God's intent is] *that at the present time, by means of the church, the angelic rulers and powers in the heavenly world might learn of His wisdom in all its different forms.*
>
> Ephesians 3:10 GNT

There is another aspect to overcoming Python. Our individual calling is part of the general calling of the Church. And whatever our unique destiny is within the whole Body, an integral part of it is to teach Python that God's wisdom is so high we cannot begin to imagine it.

It's about the glory of God.

And His delight in us.

God wants to mature us; He wants to change His relationship with us through name covenant and threshold covenant; He wants us to be His friend as well as His child; He wants us to mend history and heal the land; He wants us to move on from salvation and through the process of sanctification; He wants us to be transformed from glory to glory, glorifying Him and reflecting His glory.

God never constricts; He never wastes; He never retaliates. He has an invitation waiting for you to cross the threshold and be His friend.

But it's up to you whether you accept it. It's your call.

No matter how Python operates in your circumstances through constriction, silence, ambiguity, intimidation, torment, seduction, jealousy or sacrifice, God is still on the throne.

Let me give the last word on the subject of Python and its allied powers to the apostle Paul:

'neither death nor life, neither angels nor principalities, neither the present nor the future, nor any powers, neither height nor depth, nor anything else in all creation, will be able to separate us from the love of God that is in Christ Jesus our Lord.'

Romans 8:38–39 BSB

Love is not merely our answer to every tactic of Python, but God's answer too.

Prayer

Father God, thank You for sending Jesus as the Good Shepherd. Thank You that He guides me and pastures me, refreshes me and knows me. I thought I knew You and Him in return, but I realise I knew *about* You much more than I actually knew You. You want our love relationship in right order and I keep blocking my ears to You—whether You whisper or whether You shout. Forgive me for ignoring You and Your word.

Forgive me for agreeing with Python. Forgive me for the strain that's put on my relationship with You and with others. Forgive me for the offerings I have made to Python of myself, of others, of You. Forgive me for my complicity with others in their sacrifices to Python. Forgive me for dishonouring Python, not understanding that You gave it the right to test all my choices—and thereby indirectly blaming You. Forgive me all the ways I've tried to use a formula or a technique to cross the threshold, instead of asking You. Forgive me for my wilfulness.

Thank You for standing in harm's way and being my Shepherd and my Guide, despite my failures.

Father, Python has tempted me many times to turn from You. It knows that, when I turn to You and seek Your face with all my heart, mind and strength, I will learn the secret of overcoming and defeating it. It wants me to focus on it, instead of building an intimate love relationship with You.

It wants me to think that faith and authority render it powerless. I repent of the times I tried to declare my authority when in my ignorance I was acting counter to Your Word.

I ask You to fill my heart with Your redeemed love and to nail to the Cross of Jesus any fleshly, unregenerate love that fulfils my own desires rather than bows to Your will. Father, bring me safe across the threshold. As the Good Shepherd would lift a wounded sheep on His shoulders, lift me and heal me of all the pain, frustration and heartache that has come from not seeing Your call in my life fulfilled.

Thank You for wanting me back.

In the name of Jesus, the Good Shepherd and Gate of the Sheep. Amen.

Appendix 1

Brief Summary

PYTHON IS A FALLEN ANGEL. It is a threshold guardian and belongs to the class called the cherubim. God conferred on it the legal right to test humanity's choices as we approach thresholds, particularly any threshold into our calling. Because it is a guardian cherub whose role was to defend the threshold that only the righteous might enter, it looks for righteousness. Since faith can be credited as righteousness, it will also test for that.

Its primary tactics to squeeze our faith dry are:

1. Constriction
2. Silence and ambiguity
3. Divination
4. Intimidation
5. Seduction
6. Illness and torment
7. Demand for sacrifice
8. Jealousy

In responding to the demand for sacrifice, we are tempted to:

1. Sacrifice ourselves
2. Sacrifice others
3. Sacrifice the honour of God

Any of these brings us into complicity and covenant with Python and moves us away from God's protective cover. Because the essence of covenant is oneness, we are not truly one with God while we have a covenant with any spirit other than His Holy Spirit.

Python may accept (2) or (3) above as sufficient to cross the threshold—but these particular sacrifices set us up for retaliation by Leviathan. (1) constitutes self-sabotage: we're doing Python's work for it.

Actually, we're doing Python's work for it whenever we fail to acknowledge that Jesus is the all-sufficient sacrifice to pass any threshold.

To overcome Python, it's important to recognise that increased faith is not the answer. Love is.

The first step to overcoming Python is identifying and repenting of any false refuge or place of comfort away from God in times of disappointment. The second step is passing the test and going to God when we are next disappointed. The third step is revoking any covenant with Python that exists in our family line and renouncing our own complicity through sacrifice.

Python has allies. If it senses defeat, it may summon any of several high-level spirits whose tactics are entirely different but whose purpose is the same. These spirits include a spirit of wasting, of retaliation, of forgetting, of rejection, a vampire spirit and a spirit of armies.

Do not bind these spirits. Don't abuse, revile or call them nasty names.

Ask the Lord to rebuke them. Anyone who has dishonoured these spirits is legally liable for the penalties listed at Jude 1:9–11 and 2 Peter 2:10–12. So, don't do the 'Surely it's all done at the Cross' routine. These verses were written to believers!

And don't string out the mercy of God, either. Do what Revelation 2:16 says in veiled allusion to falling for the tactics of Python: 'Repent!'

And do it quickly.

Appendix 2

Random Stuff

THIS APPENDIX COVERS SOME QUESTIONS that have come up across the years as I have investigated Python. At the time of writing, they are my unanswerables and my hypotheticals. I put them here for your discernment and consideration.

Question 1: Does Python have something to do with the spiritual causes of hearing loss?

Certainly, hearing loss is a constriction. However, constriction alone is not enough to indicate the presence of Python. 'The narrow way' Jesus advocates we take can sometimes feel constricting.

The matter of hearing loss is in fact a complex question because the Scriptural example of hearing loss on the threshold is Simon Peter chopping off the ear of the high priest's servant. It's definitely a threshold moment—Jesus is right in the middle of being arrested—and Jesus has told him that the satan has asked to test him. But the way Jesus addressed him when He informed him of the satan's agenda is *really* interesting: *'Simon, Simon, behold, Satan has demanded permission to sift you like wheat.'* (Luke 22:31 NAS)

Jesus doesn't call him 'Peter' or 'Cephas'. He calls him 'Simon', a name that means *hear*. Its sense is a Hebrew one of *listening attentively and obeying*, not a Greek one of *registering a sound*.

Now, the high priest was Caiphas—essentially the same name as Cephas, the name Jesus gave him. Cephas is basically *threshold stone* or *cornerstone*, and Jesus gave it to Simon during a name covenant at Caesarea Philippi. Simon called Jesus 'Messiah' and, in exchange, Jesus gave him one of His own names: Cephas, *cornerstone*.

Pretty standard stuff when it comes to name exchanges. A similar thing happened when Abram became Abraham.

Now, of course, Cephas obviously doesn't displace the name Simon. This is the moment of testing 'Simon'; the time of testing 'Cephas' is yet to come in the courtyard of Caiaphas.

Simon's name goes back to Simeon, one of the sons of Jacob. At the end of Jacob's life, when he blesses his sons, he gives the birthright of the firstborn to Judah, bypassing the older brothers Reuben, Simeon and Levi. The reason Simeon lost out on this inheritance was because of violence with a sword.

So—this suggests that Simon's calling in life was to inherit what Simeon had lost by not choosing violence at a critical moment of choice. The symbolism of the 'loss of an ear' points to Simon's loss of identity and inheritance as well as his failure to repair the wounds of history traceable back to Simeon.

Jesus heals the ear of the servant—thus being the One whose mission of 'mending the world' encompasses even the violence of Jacob's sons.

But, back to my original question: does Python have something to do with the spiritual causes of hearing loss?

In a general sense, it's hard to know. But I think that in connection with names like Simon or Peter, it may well be the case.

A related question is: does Python have something to do with the spiritual causes of schizophrenia?

I believe, as a result of reading German New Medicine, that the spiritual causes of schizophrenia are two vows. One of these vows is hidden, the other is to do with listening. Or more accurately, vowing never to listen.

If the answer to 'hearing loss' is *yes* generally, rather than *yes* in very specific cases to do with very specific names, I think the answer to 'schizophrenia' is also *yes*.

Question 2: Does Python have something to do with the spiritual causes of Asperger Syndrome?

In my experience, God protects more than His Word; He protects words. Although they change in meaning across the ages, sounds retain something of the same sense. The original meaning is never entirely erased, even if it gets entirely flipped over and reversed. Of course, cultural nuances have to be taken into account, but for all that, the persistence of sense and resonance is remarkable.

All that was by way of saying that the names given to diseases have mythic overtones you'd hardly suspect. It's my view that Alzheimer's, for instance, encodes the name of a god able to interfere with memory. As for Asperger's, well 'as' is an old Teutonic word for *god* and 'per' generally retains a sense of a *beginning*, an *opening* or a *threshold* across many languages.

People who have Asperger Syndrome fear to cross boundaries to an inordinate degree. They want to know the rules. They find comfort in clearly defined laws and regulations. They hate surprises. They often get into trouble for objecting to people breaking the rules.

Sean had Asperger's. He knew that there were certain out-of-bounds areas in the school grounds and he was careful to keep away from them. One day a new sports teacher directed the class onto an oval Sean knew was classified 'out-of-bounds'. He refused to step onto it. He wouldn't move over the boundary. The furious teacher saw him as rebellious and defiant and didn't take the time to find out that, although Sean was aware of the concept of an 'exception to the rule', no one had told him this was one. No one had ever informed him that a sports teacher has the right to declare an out-of-bounds area to be in-bounds.

Because scenarios like this are so common with Asperger's, I am suspicious that the spiritual issue is Python-related.

Righteousness and justice are mega-important to those with Asperger's; the 'law' is a lifeline of security; knowledge of the rules is an enormous relief; grace is an almost incomprehensible notion.

Getting someone with Asperger's to see that 'the law' is a false refuge and repenting of it is extremely difficult. Breaking down the reliance on the rules is so terribly hard. Getting them to think about cases like that of Alton Logan, imprisoned for 26 years for a crime he not only didn't commit but that two lawyers knew he didn't, is maybe the only way. What is more important: justice for an innocent man or keeping the rule of silence in client-lawyer privilege?[37]

Question 3: Does Python have something to do with endocrine disruptors?

When I first saw the word *phthalates*, I noted the unusual set of consonants at the start: **phth**. It reminded me of the English transliterations of python-related words: mi**phth**an, for example—the defiled threshold that indicates the presence of Python. Or Je**phth**ah, the name of the judge of Israel who made a rash vow about sacrificing the first thing to come over his threshold when he returned from battle.

That particular combination of Hebrew letters (פת) is evocative of thresholds and of Python. While it isn't obvious in English that this spirit's tactics are related to its name, in Hebrew these consonants—sometimes rendered **pt**,[38] as well as **phth**—are like alarms indicating its essence and presence. Look across this list of words and think back to Python's nature, strategies and agenda:

phthn: *cobra, asp, serpent, adder, python*

phth: *hinge, something that opens*

phthm: *suddenly*

phthh: *seduce, allure, entice, lure, deceived*

phthy: *foolish, simple, gullible, seducible*

phthl: *twisting, winding, cunning, wrestling*

phthltl: *crooked, tortuous*

Phthwr: *Pethor*, home of Balaam the diviner, probably meaning *divination*

phthch: *doorway, opening, unfolding* or *appearance* (through a *door* or *gate,* or from a *womb*), *pose a riddle, expound an ambiguity*

phthchh: *drawn sword* (in sense of *suddenly appearing*)

phthr: *interpret dreams*—related to *divination*

See why I'd be suspicious of anything named **phth**alates?

Phthalates are salts or esters of phthalic acid and are used in plastics to increase their flexibility, transparency, durability and longevity. They are also found in some cosmetics, fragranced lotions, body washes, hair care products and nail polish. They are toxic and cause endocrine disruption, cancer and problems in development and reproduction.

Now, I've already said that I believe God protects words. So, although I have been unable to trace the etymology of the words phthalates and phthalic—one website suggesting it was of Greek origin and another of Persian—I reserve the right to suspect God has given us this word to tell us Python has its mitts on it.

Certainly, there are parts of the endocrine system that have names resonating of 'threshold'. The thyroid is part of the endocrine system. The name is taken from the Greek word for *shield* because, appropriately, it's a shield-shape. However, that particular Greek word isn't just a *shield*—it's also a *door*. It's the word Paul used for the *shield of faith* when he described the Armour of God. And it isn't just the *shield of faith*, it's also the *door of faith*.

And faith, of course, is exactly what Python wants to squeeze right out of us.

Thyroid problems may be an indication in the physical world of an issue with Python in the spiritual realm.

Question 4: Does Python have something to do with the spiritual causes of neck and throat problems?

There was a time when I couldn't move my neck more than the tiniest fraction. Just a few centimetres, nothing more. I can look back and see it was a threshold time. I was writing a children's novel which, while it wasn't my first book, it was the first I tried seriously to find a publisher for.

For over three months, for no discernible reason, I couldn't turn my neck at all. It was stiff and sore and just about locked into position. One day it—*finally*—occurred to me that it might be a spiritual problem. So I prayed, 'Lord, if this is an attack by an unholy spirit, could You please send it away?'

Nothing happened for about three minutes. Then I felt as if a huge cable with knots in it was being pulled out of me. The sensation would get to the knot and I'd jerk in pain. Get to another knot; jerk. Another knot; jerk. But after just a short while, I was totally free. I praised and thanked God... and went on with life.

My neck was great for a considerable while. But the issue came back. And you might think I'd go straight to the Lord. But no. I forgot. I forgot it had been a spiritual issue previously, I forgot a simple prayer had changed the matter. It took weeks before—*suddenly*—I remembered. I felt like a complete numbskull. How could I have forgotten? As I prayed again, the knotted cable came out once more.

Was it Python? I believe so.

Neck, after all, is derived from 'anaq', which corresponds to the name of the sons of Anak—the giants who intimidated the majority of the spies surveying the Promised Land. The word 'anaq' originally had the sense of *throttle, choke, strangle* or *noose*, though in later times it apparently came to denote things a lot less threatening like *necklace* and *pendant*. These giants were descended from the Nephilim and were agents of the spirit of Python.

Now, for me, the most significant part of this episode was not the neck pain—problematic as that was, in retrospect, it was actually the forgetting that was the bigger issue.

Now forgetting is not a tactic of Python. Rather, it's a tactic of the spirit of forgetting—an ally of Python.

The spirit of forgetting is one that dismembers truth. The opposite of *remember* is, in fact, *dismember* and the Greek word, 'aletheia', derives from *not forget*.

And so, from that, we can tell one of the best approaches to overcoming the spirit of forgetting is to ask God for the re-integration of truth in our lives.

Appendix 3
Common Symbols of Python

THIS LIST, WHILE REASONABLY COMPREHENSIVE, is by no means exhaustive. God will often highlight the presence of Python in your life by using 'dark speech'; that is, veiled language, parables, dream imagery and riddles to communicate its return into your life. Riddles and ambiguity, we need to remember, were not created by Python. It simply uses them against us. Nor are any numbers or symbols the property of Python. They are stolen. Even a serpent entwined on a pole was originally God's sign for healing.

Of course, a single example of the following is not necessarily indicative of Python. It's important to look for a pattern, not an isolated instance. A cluster of the following would generally indicate the specific activity of Python, providing it contains one element from the first line. Otherwise, a cluster would generally indicate the activity of another of the threshold spirits.

- serpent, cobra, asp, adder, viper, rooster, cock
- typhoon, whirlwind, hurricane, cyclone
- north, north star
- firstborn
- door, opening, threshold, hinge

- bridges, piers, pylons, boundaries, frontiers, gates
- fortune-teller, sooth-sayer, diviner
- door-keeper, gate-keeper, watchman, guard
- sphinx or three-headed dog Cerberus
- symbolic staff of medical profession
- heel, foot, bruising
- names like Peter or Jacob or ones starting with 'Jan-' or 'Cleo-' or Thomas; there are many threshold-related names but these seem to be more particularly associated with Python than with its allied spirits
- the letter *E*, the word 'if'
- double face, two heads
- twisted cord, wick
- neck, necklace, pendant, scarf, noose, strangling, choking
- theft of 5 or 101
- tiler of Freemasonry and other similar Lodges
- yoke, yoga or any word associated with yoga
- images like Darth Vader, Tyler Durden, Scylla and Charybdis, sirens of Greek mythology, Medusa, giants
- cherubim, swords

Appendix 4
The Silver Chair

A discursive review of the fantasy novel from The Chronicles of Narnia
with particular reference to Python and other spirits of the threshold.
Please look back at the end of the Introduction before reading.

Once upon a time, in my very late teens, I discovered *The Chronicles of Narnia* and read the entire series in a single week. Way back then, I would probably have rated the fourth book, *The Silver Chair,* a mere two stars out of five. But only because I was feeling generous and I was still in the halo of the third book, *The Voyage of the Dawn Treader.*

Some time in the intervening decades, *The Silver Chair* moved from the bottom of my ratings to the top. I mean the *very* top. Today I'd give it more than five stars. Its rise has been steady; modest at first, it eventually came to float in and out of my Top 10 for a while. Now it's a serious contender for the all-time Number 1 spot.

My change of heart began when I attended a L'Abri conference featuring Jerram Barrs and Wim Rietkirk at the University of Queensland sometime in the early eighties. One of them—I think it was Rietkirk—quoted at length from the scene where Rilian, Puddleglum and the children face off the Green Witch as she strums her enchantment of befuddlement in the Underworld. I can't remember exactly what they said but it changed my appreciation of the whole book. It stopped being one of my least favourite books and began its slow ascendancy.

Then came the BBC series with Tom Baker (the fourth Doctor in the *Doctor Who* television series) as Puddleglum the marshwiggle. Such a respectabiggle portrayal! I liked the series so much, the book again made a jump in my estimation. (I even liked the bit they added when Eustace talks to the dragon—such a perfect touch!)

Then I started to write books of my own. I loved two of the *Narnia* books, hated two and felt the other three were middling. It was an enormous surprise to me when, as I started to write, I found myself wanting to fill in the 'missing' story set on Ettinsmoor! Until I was half way into chapter 1 of *Merlin's Wood*, I had no idea I thought Narnia was incomplete, let alone that its incompleteness was connected with a story centred on Ettinsmoor. Fortunately, good sense prevailed and my story shifted location to another planet entirely! However, faint echoes of my flirtation with Ettinsmoor can be still be found throughout the story.

As a result of this experience, I realised something deep in my spirit connected with something deep in this story, despite my superficial equivocation about liking it.

The huge leap forward came as a result of two books: *Planet Narnia* and *Green Suns and Faërie*.

I love *Planet Narnia*. I think it's a brilliant and incisive investigation into a code that the author, Michael Ward, believes is used throughout the *Narnia* series as an overall thematic unity. His hypothesis is the seven books of the *Chronicles* are based around the seven medieval planets—Mercury, Venus, Mars, Jupiter, Saturn, the Sun and the Moon. These of course are not the modern planets.

Now genius as I think Ward's insight is, I also happen to think it's wrong. In a very subtle way. As much as the difference between the north pole and the north magnetic pole.

I was succumbing to the charms of its central premise—that the *Narnia* series is based around the seven medieval planets—when I was brought up short by an obvious error. *The Silver Chair* is not, in my view, themed around the Moon. It's themed around giants—and as far as classical mythology goes, the planet associated with giants has never been the Moon. (Different if it's Norse mythology, where Mani the moon is the giant who captures the children who become the basis of the *Jack and Jill* rhyme. But Ward presents his findings based on classical scholarship, not Teutonic.) In Roman mythology, the giant has to be the Titan, Chronus—identified with Saturn—or his son, Jupiter.

In fact, 40% of the chapters of *The Silver Chair* directly deal with giants or with giants' work. I felt Ward had been swayed by the word *silver* and its ubiquitous poetic association with the moon.

Now despite Ben Jonson describing the moon goddess Cynthia[39] as seated in a silver chair, I still don't believe the story is lunar-themed. I don't think Lewis took his inspiration from Jonson. Rather I believe the silverness of the chair is another of Jack's (many) tips of the hat to his friend and colleague, Ronald Tolkien.

In the collection of scholarly articles, *Green Suns and Faërie*, Verlyn Flieger writes of JRR Tolkien's reworking of a Breton folktale on a variant theme of the Orpheus legend—the Greek hero who, when his beloved dies, journeys to the Underworld to bring her back.

This Breton folktale features the Corrigan—a faery woman who sits on a silver chair, rules an underworld and seeks to lure a hero to her dark realm. Straightaway here is an entire plot thread of *The Silver Chair*.[40] The story doesn't end well for the hero of the folktale, so Lewis' variant on a variant is more in line with the happily-ever-after of the medieval poem, *Sir Orfeo*. (Yes, *The Lord of The Rings* fans might just recognise this poem as another of Tolkien's obsessions—his translation of this medieval work is collected with *Sir Gawain and the Green Knight* as well as *Pearl*.)

The alignment of the plot of *The Silver Chair* with the Breton folktale suggests that *silver* has far more to do with Tolkien's description of the Corrigan's seat than any lunar aspect.

The Corrigan is a fairly obscure denizen of the lands of elfin. I suspect her name reminded Lewis of the Morrighan—the war goddess of Ulster, the land of his birth. The Morrighan is said to be the forerunner of the witch-queen Morgan le Fay in Arthurian romance. This is significant because Lewis was seriously tempted to name the White Witch 'Morgan' and not 'Jadis', as early drafts of *The Magician's Nephew* indicate. The inspiration of the Corrigan as a distant relative of the Morrighan is, I think, alluded to in the distant relationship between the witches of the north to Jadis.

Jadis has, like Aslan, echoes of Norse naming. (Yes, I know, the alleged inspiration for Aslan's name: Turkish cigarettes called Aslans with pictures of lions on them. *Tales of the Arabian Nights* with lions, aslans, in them. Hmm. For a man self-admittedly 'crazed with northern-ness'? When Aslan from Old Norse is *god of the land*?!) There are several possible translations for Jadis from Old Norse, but I'm inclined to go with *ironwood witch-mother*. Which probably explains the appearance of Fenris Ulf instead of Maugrim in the American editions: because he too comes from the legendary ironwood of Norse mythology.

I'm continually surprised by the bizarre tendency of those who write about Lewis to overlook the Old Icelandic language. There are too many allusions to Norse mythology to look south to the Mediterranean for the answers in my view. Sure, there may be wordplay involving Latin or Turkish in the snow-swirled landscape of Narnia, but I consider this akin to the multi-lingual puns Jesus made when He was talking about the Evil Eye or the multitude of cross-cultural allusions Paul layered into the Armour of God.

So, heading north, I will reiterate that giants dominate the tale of *The Silver Chair*, far more than silvery things or watery things or lunar things. And in Norse mythology, the giants are the thurses, the rises and the jotuns; they're related to the ettins or eotens from which Tolkien derived the name, ents. Even in Irish folklore, the Red Ettin is a giant of the Jack-and-the-Beanstalk school. Here's where the name Ettinsmoor comes into its own: it's the high moorland of the giants. Fits nicely. It's probably based on the Borders area of Scotland, since the folktale of the giant of the broch of Edinshall (*edin* being a variant of *ettin*) is about a rock-throwing game—tossing a boulder from the top of the hill into the River Whiteadder. (And, yes, of course there is a stream called the Blackadder nearby.)

Now rock-throwing giants are the very thing that Eustace, Jill and Puddleglum encounter as they cross the northern wastes. On Ettinsmoor they observe ettins. How nicely neat.

Now in Norse mythology, gnomes and giants are occasionally confused. Thus, if it's permissible to add in the chapters about the gnomes to the count of the giants, over 50% of the book is devoted to the big guys. To return to the premise of Michael Ward's book, *Planet Narnia*—that the stories are themed around the medieval planets—I would like to suggest that his overall idea is right, if the specific is wrong. The giant planet is not the Moon but Jupiter. And in medieval times Jupiter was equated to Thor. Both wield thunderbolts, for the obvious parallel.

We refer to Thor all the time, even though very few of us are conscious of it. When the Germanic tribes adopted the Roman weekly calendar, they replaced the Roman gods with their own. Latin 'dies Iovis', day of Jupiter, was renamed 'Þonares dagaz', *Thor's day,* from which stems our modern English word, *Thursday*.

Yes, Thursday is named after this feisty hammer-wielding giant. And herein lies, I think, Lewis' clever gamesmanship and mastery of words. *The Silver Chair* is themed around Thursday, not the Moon. Moreover, it's more than a nod to Thor/Jupiter but also encompasses the thurses of Norse mythology. (Not forgetting *thur* from old Gaelic is *strong*.)

As it happens, the medieval planets correspond to the Days of the Week. So I believe Michael Ward in *Planet Narnia* was utterly, superlatively, outstandingly right in his overall theory while still being wrong in important specific details. (Because it's a closed system, one error means there have to be at least two. Another involves *The Voyage of the Dawn Treader* which should be aligned with Wednesday and Woden, who in medieval thinking corresponded to Mercury, the god of travellers. For me, this association of *The Voyage of the Dawn Treader* and Woden/Mercury is clearly attested by a tiny detail: the silver sea or lily lake sailed by Reepicheep as he approaches the dawn at the end of the world. The lily sea appears in a myth about Mercury: he lies in wait for the nymph Chloris who spreads lilies, roses and violets after the sun as it rose.)

Now all this cleverness on the part of Jack Lewis was admirable and academic, and scholarly and wonderful. But it certainly wasn't enough to catapult *The Silver Chair* so far up it has come to rival my all-time favourite story. And when I'm talking favourites, I mean in terms of emotional satisfaction, not intellectual esteem.

What overturned my entire view of the story was my study of Python and threshold covenants. As I've worked on understanding them and listing their symptoms, I realised *The Silver Chair* is a threshold story without peer.

For a start, it's a portal fantasy. That means it's about doorways to other worlds. Now there are a lot of portal fantasies around but that doesn't mean all of them qualify as tales of threshold covenants. The hard-to-miss aspect of *The Silver Chair* when it comes to thresholds is that Python actually appears—as a stupendous, constricting green serpent.

That might be enough but there's far more. The letter *E*, so famous at Delphi, appears at a moment of significant choice. Later it turns out to be the actual doorway to the Underworld.

In addition, the spirit of forgetting is symbolised by the tremendous number of memory issues faced by Jill.

The spirit of wasting doesn't appear but both the wasteland and many wasted opportunities are present. Neither does the spirit of rejection appear but there are many incidents featuring rejection. Likewise, the spirit of backlash doesn't appear but the destruction of the Underworld after the death of the Witch may indicate its presence.

The vampire spirit, surprisingly, is a help to the heroes: it's represented by the owls, who are symbolic of the original taloned soul-huntress of the night, Lilith—the forerunner of the modern idea of the vampire.

The Python figure—the witchy Lady of the Green Kirtle—is allied with giants who are out to make a meal of the heroes. Seduced into ease and comfort, the heroes seem to have an unconscious urge to sacrifice themselves to these jovial, accommodating threshold guardians. Ironically-named, these Gentle Giants of Harfang Castle[41] combine aspects of the Red Ettin (but without the 'fie-fi-fo-fum' chant), the giant of *Jack and the Beanstalk* but with more civilised manners and the intimidating biblical sons of Anak.

The castle of these giants is on the threshold of the way into the Underworld—the place where the destiny of the heroes awaits. Other obvious thresholds within the story include the huge and crumbling bridge which crosses a river. For a medievalist like Lewis, the trope of crossing water signals a passage over a boundary into fairyland. Indeed, the heroes immediately encounter The Lady of the Green Kirtle who is accompanied by a mysterious, silent black knight. Green is the traditional colour of fairyland and magic in old folklore.

The Python figure, disguised as the Lady of the Green Kirtle, offers ambiguous information to the heroes. The Black Knight is the enchanted prince, Rilian, the son of King Caspian.[42] The Lady has struck him dumb: he maintains total silence and, except for one hour a day, has no idea who he is. He suffers a theft of both identity and destiny.

Most significantly in terms of threshold covenant, he is the son who is brainwashed and appointed to oppose his own father as the head of an invading army—a role that corresponds to the action of a Janissary spirit.[43]

The madness of Prince Rilian is a delirium caused by magical imposition. Delirium may be a wordplay on his name. The letters 'l' and 'r' are often substituted across languages; reversing them Rilian becomes 'lirian', an assonance with *delirium*. Delirium comes from the phrase 'de lira', *off the furrow*. 'Lira' may be the source of the name Lear, the mad king of Shakespeare's famous play, since alternative mythological spellings include Leir, Lir and Llyr. The city of Leicester is said to be named after an ancient British king who was buried in a temple to Janus on the river Soar. Janus is a threshold god, traditionally the most ancient Roman deity—in charge of doorways as well as the first month of the year. In addition, *furrow* may be an allusion, although undoubtedly unintentional, to one of the Biblical sons of

Anak, those giant allies of Python. Talmai's name comes from a root for furrow.[44]

There are much more direct insinuations of Python, however. The unnamed Lady of the Green Kirtle represents the unnamed Pythia or Pythoness—the priestess who functioned as the oracle at Delphi. The Pythia's trance-like state as she inhales the hallucinatory vapours of the underground crevice is reflected in the trance-like state which afflicts the heroes as they inhale the hallucinatory fumes of the Green Witch's fire. The message over the entrance to the shrine of Delphi, *Know thyself*, is as ambiguous as the oracle's own utterances. It suggests, in one sense, that knowledge is relative. This is the precise message of the Green Witch as she conjures a glamour and seeks to persuade the heroes that the sun is an illusion, based on the idea of a lamp and that Aslan is an imaginary projection of a cat.

Now all these things pertain to threshold covenant but the real surety that this is a major theme of the book is that it so strongly features name covenant. Name and threshold covenant go together. You can't have the second without the first. They're designed to reinforce each other.

The name covenant that should be—and is—evident throughout the story is Clive Staples Lewis. It's more about his nickname Jack than anything else but his more formal name is not neglected.

Let's check out Clive Staples Lewis to see how the name covenant operates.

Clive derives from Latin 'clivus', meaning *cliff* or *slope of a hill*.

Staples, bent pieces of metal with pointed ends, originally comes from Old English, 'stapol', meaning *a pillar, a post, a pole* or *a spike*.

Lewis is a Welsh name meaning lion and deriving from the name of the Celtic god of light, Llew Llaw Gyffes, *the Lion of the Steady Hand*.

Jack is often considered to be a nickname from John which is usually given as meaning *God is gracious*. However, there are three folkloric appearances of Jack significant for the *Narnia* series.

1. Jack is the name commonly used in English folklore for a satyr or faun.[45]

2. Jack is the name of the fatherless boy who outwits a giant in the fairytale, *Jack and the Beanstalk*.

3. Jack is the name of the boy in the nursery rhyme, *Jack and Jill*, who goes to fetch a pail of water but falls down and breaks his crown.

The story starts with Eustace Scrubb and Jill Pole fleeing from school bullies through an old gate and finding themselves in Aslan's Country, close to the edge of a staggeringly high cliff. In that single sentence we can find veiled references to Clive, to Staples and to Lewis.

Eustace is the English form of Eustachys, meaning *good spike*, though it's usually translated quite loosely as *fruitful* or *ear of corn*. *Spike* is of course a root meaning of 'staple', as is *pole*—Jill's surname.[46] Both of these names allude to Staples, the surname of Lewis' mother's mother.

Several competing stories account for the use of the name Aslan in the *Chronicles* to identify the great king and lord of the wood who rules all Narnia. Regardless of which of the rival versions is true,[47] the Turkish name, 'Aslan', shares a common meaning with the Welsh name, 'Lewis'. They are both words for *lion*.

Clive, as I've already mentioned, derives from the Latin word for *cliff*.

So, by the end of the second chapter, Lewis had already shone a spotlight onto every part of his official name.

His preferred name, Jack, is referenced regularly—and always indirectly—throughout the rest of the story.

Eustace falls off the cliff and, after meeting up with Aslan, Jill is blown to Narnia by the lion's breath. She tumbles after Eustace, arriving with a big watery splash. Shades of the nursery rhyme, *Jack and Jill*. Here's the first allusion to Jack—the name Lewis gave himself as a pre-schooler. Such subtle references recur through the story, but never in an overt way.

Now because this story continually evokes mythic resonances of the name Jack, it naturally has giants. Because what else does Jack face in the most enduring fairytale of all about a boy of that name? A giant, of course! At the top of a beanstalk.

Lewis had always been fascinated by the foes of his namesake. He wrote passionately of Gawain from *Sir Gawain and the Green Knight* (the same medieval poem that Tolkien translated) and the ettins that were blowing after him in that story. The Green Knight of the tale is half-ettin himself, his unnamed wife has a green girdle and appears to be a student of Morgan le Fay.

So, it is no surprise to find gusts of this great medieval poem, *Sir Gawain and the Green Knight*, all the way through *The Silver Chair*. It isn't far from the Lady of the Green Girdle to the Lady of the Green Kirtle, after all, especially when both of whom are artists of ambiguity and deceit.

Nor is it entirely impossible that Puddleglum, the tall, green and gallant Marshwiggle, is a rustic version of the tall, green and chivalrous Green Knight himself. Pessimism might characterise Puddleglum instead of the ever-cheerful countenance of the Green Knight, but both of them are catalysts who push the heroes of their respective tales towards climactic choices.

Even before Eustace and Jill encounter the half-ettinish Puddleglum on Ettinsmoor, their choices have been significant. The lion's breath which propels them into Narnia harks back to the ettins blowing after Gawain—an image that Lewis found compelling.

The wind is a hidden element in Narnia: the initial letters of the names of the seven lords whom Caspian is seeking in *The Voyage of the Dawn Treader*—Bern, Octesian, Restimar, Rhoop, Argoz, Revilian, Mavramorn—taken in order spell out 'borrar(u)m', Latin for *of the north wind*.[48]

Perhaps we may consider them 'Boreans': *knights of the north wind*.

Here finally we have a link between the oracle at Delphi and Lewis' self-admitted state of 'crazed with northern-ness'. It was thought that Apollo, alone amongst the Greek gods of Olympus, was also revered by the Hyperboreans—the giants who lived in the land beyond the north wind. Once a year, Apollo was said to go far to the north to receive their worship, and at that time, the

Delphic oracle closed down, since the god of the shrine was considered absent and away travelling.[49]

But there's also a link between Delphi and Thor. The Greek equivalent of Jupiter is Zeus and their Norse equivalent is Thor. Zeus wanted to locate the centre of the earth. So, according to legend, he sent two eagles from the ends of the world. Launched at the same moment and travelling at the same speed, they met at Delphi. Zeus, wanting a more precise GPS coordinate, threw a stone from the sky and where it fell was considered the omphalos, the navel of the earth. The heaven-sent stone itself was the navelstone—the Greek rival to the 'eben ha-shetiyah'.

Lewis is often said to have developed the *Narnia* series as an allegory with a specific Christian message. Many people believe he was inspired to smuggle doctrinal truths into children's fantasy adventures and deliver the gospel that way. He repeatedly denied this allegation. And anyone who thinks about it for more than a moment should realise how absurd the idea is. A talking lion, a witch who uses Turkish Delight as a supreme temptation, a wardrobe which erratically functions as an entrance to another world, a faun who likes sardines on toast, a realm in which it's always winter and never Christmas—does any of this sound remotely like a recipe for presenting the gospel? You can't see what's coming in *The Lion, the Witch and the Wardrobe*—certainly not like *Pilgrim's Progress* where there's no ambiguity about Giant Despair, Faithful, Obstinate, Pliant, Evangelist, Lord Hate-good or any of the many others whose characters are obvious from their names.

Lewis maintained that his inspiration for *The Lion, the Witch and the Wardrobe* was a picture that had recurred in his mind's eye from the time he was a teenager. It was an image of a faun, standing near a lamp-post and holding an umbrella and some parcels. Several decades went by before he decided to write about this faun. And, according to his own testimony, as soon as he did, 'the Lion came bounding in.'

The faun, as previously indicated, points to the name 'Jack'. And the lion to the name 'Lewis'.

The Silver Chair may be, as indicated previously, Lewis' sacrificial offering to God of his own cherished ambition to be a poet—since the silver chair was the coveted prize awarded to the top bard in a Welsh eisteddfod.

From start to finish, *The Chronicles of Narnia* is a wrestle with various names: with 'Clive' and 'Staples', with 'Lewis' and 'Jack'. However, it is also a tussle with 'Hamilton', a pseudonym he assumed for the publication of his early poetry.

Hamilton was his mother's maiden name. I'm very fortunate I share that name, as well as a paternal ancestry going back to Northern Ireland. It gives me a close insight into the name covenant defilements Lewis struggled to excise. As an Irish name, Hamilton is considerably more complex than its Scots counterpart. It can be an anglicisation of hUrmoltaigh or Tromulty!

I've even seen a list once with a variant form starting with a Z. I'd love to find that website again. The reason I'm so keen to look at the list is because, once you realise old Celtic Z is pronounced as a Y, it reveals a hidden secret. The pronunciation of the first syllable of the Irish version of 'Hamilton' is 'yom'.

And 'yom' is the Hebrew word for *day*.

The subtle obsession with time throughout *The Chronicles of Narnia* is one I share in my own fiction. 'What exactly is a *day*?'

I have to say I think Ralph Waldo Emerson nailed it in more than one way when he wrote: 'No one suspects the days to be gods.'

Having changed spiritual entities into conceptual abstractions, we don't realise that naming the days after gods is an exercise in dedication as serious as any human baptismal ceremony.

Naming is about identity. As a consequence, it's also about destiny.

Names are unbelievably powerful. They can bless and they can destroy. As I've worked with people suffering dissociative identity disorder as a result of ritual abuse, I've repeatedly found it's about an unauthorised name they've been given. The fragmentation of self is as much dissociative name disorder as identity disorder.

Lewis paved the way for us. I believe the reason his books are so attractive to the souls of so many children, over seventy years after they were first published, is because they reassure us spiritually. Here we have stories that don't give us a formula but show us a template, based around Lewis' own name, for the defeat of the witches—the yiddeoni, the hamingjur, the fylgjur, the familiar spirits—of our ancestry.

The spiritual theme of *The Silver Chair* says: 'Python can be defeated.'

Not only that, but the Days who seem to be abstractions for a calendar but are in fact planetary gods—the world-rulers of this present darkness—yes, they too can be defeated. And if world-rulers can be, then any cosmic power can.

Moreover, there's a sense within us this is not just a story—deep within our spirits, we know that Lewis can't have got this right unless he had already traversed this spiritual landscape himself and reached its far side.

So, we take his testimony and know we can pass over the threshold and arrive in Aslan's Country.

We are invited to come 'further up and further in' into ever deeper intimacy with the *God of the Land*.

Endnotes

1 The Hebrew word, 'pethen', פתן, directly appears six times in Scripture.

Deuteronomy 32:33 NAS—'...*the deadly poison of cobras.*'
Job 20:14 NAS—'...*the venom of cobras.*'
Job 20:16 NAS—'...*the poison of cobras.*'
Psalm 58:4 NAS—'...*a deaf cobra that stops...*'
Psalm 91:13 NAS—'...*upon the lion and the cobra...*'
Isaiah 11:8 NAS—'...*by the hole of the cobra...*'

2 Hebrew has no vowels, so the key consonants are **p**(h)**t**(h)**n** which appear in both 'pethen' and 'miphtan'. English translations do not describe 'miphtan' as *defiled*. The word is simply rendered *threshold*. However, another word can also be used for *threshold*: 'kaph'. I believe from an examination of their contexts that these different words describe an ordinary (*blessed*) threshold and a *defiled* threshold and are meant to be distinguished from each other. There are only eight Scriptural occurrences of miphtan, מפתן. Of these, the first five are *defiled* thresholds. The eighth doesn't make sense unless it too is a defiled threshold, since it would contradict injunctions relating to ordinary thresholds.

1 Samuel 5:4 NAS—'...*cut off on the threshold...*'
1 Samuel 5:5 NAS—'...*tread on the threshold of Dagon...*'
Ezekiel 9:3 NAS—'...*the threshold of the temple...*'
Ezekiel 10:4 NAS—'...*from the cherub to the threshold of the temple...*'
Ezekiel 10:18 NAS—'...*departed from the threshold of the temple...*'
Ezekiel 46:2 NAS—'...*he shall worship at the threshold of the gate...*'
Ezekiel 47:1 NAS—'...*under the threshold of the house...*'
Zephaniah 1:9 NAS—'...*who leap on the threshold...*'

3 'Staircase wit', meaning a retort that occurs to your mind once you have left and are heading down a stairwell.

4 Abarim Publications, abarim-publications.com/Meaning/Pethor (accessed 16 November 2016)

5 For the sake of finishing Butler's own thoughts on what his experience means, here is the rest of his devotional thought:

Now, of course, the flesh told me to retaliate. I'd just gotten married and had no money. My wife didn't have a job. But the Word of God said that vengeance belongs to the Lord. So I could do one of two things: Follow the flesh or follow the Word. I followed the Word.

I later went to work for a major oil company in a similar type of position and they closed down seven months later. Then God gave me a tremendous job with major computer firm. Each time I was forced to change jobs, I was blessed with another one. Because of my excellent performance, I was in a position to move into management. At about that time, the Lord told me to 'quit and go to Bible school.' I obeyed God and went to Bible school. While in school, my wife and I received a financial miracle every 30–45 days. God provided for us supernaturally while we were students. We had debt when we arrived at Bible school, but we graduated debt-free! God sent us out into the ministry debt-free.

When you live a life of obedience to God, there is nothing man or man's systems can do to keep you down. You may have a setback here and there. But if you stick with the Word, the end result will be nothing but blessings for you and yours.

6   Or, when we've undertaken a multi-year course such as Caroline did, its strike is usually in the last month to six weeks.

7   See *God's Poetry: The Identity and Destiny Encoded in Your Name*, Armour Books 2012

8   They look closer in English than they actually are in Hebrew. The word for a threshold *angel*, 'cherub', starts with a 'kaph', K, while chereb starts with a hei, CH or H. There is obviously a strong poetic link, however, between the two: the alternate name for Sinai is Horeb—which is the same word as 'chereb'. While 'chereb' is usually translated *waste* or *wasteland* in this instance, Horeb could just as legitimately be translated *mountain of the sword (of the cherubim)*. It is contrasted, in Hebrews 12:22, with the *mountain of myriad angels*.

9   This ancient sentinel who demanded the answer to a riddle is in many ways similar to the monstrous watchdog that guarded the gates to Hades, the Greek version of the Underworld. Cerberus— the offspring of Typhon and Echidna—had a mane, along with the feet of a lion, the tail of a snake and three heads. These heads were sometimes depicted as belonging to dogs or sometimes, as in the Serapis cult, belonging to a lion, a dog and a wolf.

10   Accompanied, apparently by Timothy as well as Luke, since Luke writes 'we' in verse 16.

11   Acts 16:7–40 NAS:

> *'After they came to Mysia, they were trying to go into Bithynia, and the Spirit of Jesus did not permit them; and passing by Mysia, they came down to Troas. A vision appeared to Paul in the night: a man of Macedonia was standing and appealing to him, and saying, "Come over to Macedonia and help us." When he had seen the vision, immediately we sought to go into Macedonia, concluding that God had called us to preach the gospel to them.*
>
> *So putting out to sea from Troas, we ran a straight course to Samothrace, and on the day following to Neapolis; and from there to Philippi, which is a leading city of the district of Macedonia, a Roman colony; and we were staying in this city for some days...*
>
> *It happened that as we were going to the place of prayer, a slave-girl having a spirit of divination met us, who was bringing her masters much profit by fortune-telling. Following after Paul and us, she kept crying out, saying, "These men are bond-servants of the Most High God, who are proclaiming to you the way of salvation." She continued doing this for many days. But Paul was greatly annoyed, and turned and said to the spirit, "I command you in the name of Jesus Christ to come out of her!" And it came out at that very moment.*
>
> *But when her masters saw that their hope of profit was gone, they seized Paul and Silas and dragged them into the market place before the authorities, and when they had brought them to the chief magistrates, they said, "These men are throwing our city into confusion, being Jews, and are proclaiming customs which it is not lawful for us to accept or to observe, being Romans."*
>
> *The crowd rose up together against them, and the chief magistrates tore their robes off them and proceeded to order them to be beaten with rods. When they had struck them with many blows, they threw them into prison, commanding the jailer to guard them securely; and he, having received such a command, threw them into the inner prison and fastened their feet in the stocks.*
>
> *But about midnight Paul and Silas were praying and singing hymns of praise to God, and the prisoners were listening to them; and suddenly there came a great earthquake, so that the foundations of the prison house were shaken; and immediately all the doors were opened and*

everyone's chains were unfastened. When the jailer awoke and saw the prison doors opened, he drew his sword and was about to kill himself, supposing that the prisoners had escaped. But Paul cried out with a loud voice, saying, "Do not harm yourself, for we are all here!" And he called for lights and rushed in, and trembling with fear he fell down before Paul and Silas, and after he brought them out, he said, "Sirs, what must I do to be saved?"

They said, "Believe in the Lord Jesus, and you will be saved, you and your household." And they spoke the word of the Lord to him together with all who were in his house. And he took them that very hour of the night and washed their wounds, and immediately he was baptised, he and all his household. And he brought them into his house and set food before them, and rejoiced greatly, having believed in God with his whole household.

Now when day came, the chief magistrates sent their policemen, saying, "Release those men." And the jailer reported these words to Paul, saying, "The chief magistrates have sent to release you. Therefore come out now and go in peace." But Paul said to them, "They have beaten us in public without trial, men who are Romans, and have thrown us into prison; and now are they sending us away secretly? No indeed! But let them come themselves and bring us out." The policemen reported these words to the chief magistrates. They were afraid when they heard that they were Romans, and they came and appealed to them, and when they had brought them out, they kept begging them to leave the city. They went out of the prison and entered the house of Lydia, and when they saw the brethren, they encouraged them and departed.'

12   Jentezen Franklin, *The Spirit of Python: Exposing Satan's Plan to Squeeze the Life out of You*, Charisma House 2013

13   Even this mention of brass is a significant detail. For the Hebrews, the word for *brass* is 'nechushah', related to *bronze*, 'nechash', related to *serpent*, 'nachash'.

14   A navelstone is a religious artefact which symbolically marks the 'centre of the earth'. Such centres are cultural lodestones and can be found in most continents. For the Jews as well as medieval Christians, the centre of the earth was Jerusalem.

For the ancient Greeks, however, the centre of the earth was at Delphi. This location had been determined by Zeus, the chief of the gods of Olympus. In an early scientific experiment, he had launched two eagles from the opposite ends of the world. The birds set off simultaneously and flew at equal speed. Their paths had crossed above the general vicinity of Delphi. To then determine the exact spot where the earth's centre lay, Zeus threw a stone from the sky to see where it fell. This stone allegedly later became the symbol of Apollo, of the sacred Oracle and more generally of the region of Delphi.

15   Reflecting four uses of 'if' in Philippians 2:1—'...*if there is any encouragement in Christ, if there is any consolation of love, if there is any fellowship of the Spirit, if any affection and compassion...*' (NAS)

16   Wikipedia recognises this: https://en.wikipedia.org/wiki/Omphalos

17   See *God's Pageantry: The Threshold Guardians and the Covenant Defender*, Armour Books 2014

18   I need a whole book to explain that statement, so I'm not going to even try at this point. I'll merely say that the literary design of John's gospel is in matched episodic pairs—undoubtedly inspired by the form of Hebrew poetry known as chiasmus. So, to fully understand what John is saying, it's vital to find the corresponding matched scene at the end of the gospel. A preliminary discussion on this literary design can be found in *God's Pottery: The Sea of Names and the Pierced Inheritance*, Armour Books 2016. I hope to be able to write an entire book on this subject eventually, as it is the most lusciously elegant and beautiful literary device, complementing its masterful mathematical design. (See: Maarten Menken, *Numerical Literary Techniques in John—The Fourth Evangelist's Use of Numbers of Words and Syllables*, Brill 1985)

19   jewishstudies.eteacherbiblical.com/bethesda-pool-jerusalem-shrine-asclepius/

20   See *Online Etymology Dictionary*. Search for: *syu-

21   This idea of binding ourselves to the Lord is the notion behind the admonition, '*Wait for the Lord*' in Psalm 27:14. In a different way, it is also the notion behind the Irish hymn genre known as loricas or breastplate songs. As, for example, in the famous lorica attributed to St Patrick, *The Deer's Cry*, in the evocative translation of CF Alexander:

I bind unto myself today
The strong name of the Trinity,
By invocation of the same,
The Three in One and One in Three.

I bind this day to me for ever,
By power of faith, Christ's Incarnation;
His baptism in the Jordan River;
His death on cross for my salvation;
His bursting from the spicèd tomb;
His riding up the heavenly way;
His coming at the day of doom;
I bind unto myself today.

I bind unto myself the power
Of the great love of the Cherubim;
The sweet 'Well done' in judgment hour;
The service of the Seraphim,
Confessors' faith, Apostles' word,
The Patriarchs' prayers, the Prophets' scrolls,
All good deeds done unto the Lord,
And purity of virgin souls.

I bind unto myself today
The virtues of the starlit heaven,
The glorious sun's life-giving ray,
The whiteness of the moon at even,
The flashing of the lightning free,
The whirling wind's tempestuous shocks,
The stable earth, the deep salt sea,
Around the old eternal rocks.

I bind unto myself today
The power of God to hold and lead,
His eye to watch, His might to stay,
His ear to hearken to my need.
The wisdom of my God to teach,
His hand to guide, His shield to ward,
The word of God to give me speech,
His heavenly host to be my guard.

Against the demon snares of sin,
The vice that gives temptation force,
The natural lusts that war within,
The hostile men that mar my course;
Or few or many, far or nigh,
In every place and in all hours
Against their fierce hostility,
I bind to me these holy powers.

Against all Satan's spells and wiles,
Against false words of heresy,
Against the knowledge that defiles,
Against the heart's idolatry,
Against the wizard's evil craft,
Against the death-wound and the burning
The choking wave and the poisoned shaft,
Protect me, Christ, till Thy returning.

Christ be with me, Christ within me,
Christ behind me, Christ before me,
Christ beside me, Christ to win me,
Christ to comfort and restore me,
Christ beneath me, Christ above me,
Christ in quiet, Christ in danger,
Christ in hearts of all that love me,
Christ in mouth of friend and stranger.

I bind unto myself the name,
The strong name of the Trinity;
By invocation of the same.
The Three in One, and One in Three,
Of whom all nature hath creation,
Eternal Father, Spirit, Word:
Praise to the Lord of my salvation,
salvation is of Christ the Lord.

22 Also spelled 'tetractys'.

23 Plutarch, the same high priest of Python Apollo who wrote *On the E at Delphi*, revealed this in an essay about Isis and Osiris. Much of what we know about the place of Isis and Osiris in Egyptian religion comes from Plutarch—which, for a modern parallel, is about the same as relying on the Dalai Lama for the secrets of the Sikh faith.

24 This also happens to be arranged in a musical notation which includes the octave and the perfect fifth.

25 Susanne Kries, *Skandinavisch-schottische Sprachbeziehungen im Mittelalter: Der altnordische Lehneinfluss*, University Press of Southern Denmark 2003

26 Hebrew words related to these names are:

'angq—*neck, long neck, necklace, collar, strangling, choking*
chanaq—*to be narrow, to throttle, to choke to death, ornaments of a wreath*
'anak—*lead weight, plumb*

The name Ahiman ('achicyman) may mean: *my brother is a gift* or *who is my brother?* or *my brother is like me*, that is, *a twin*

To try to uncover the meaning of this name for one of the sons of Anak, the following elements may need to be taken into account:

The word, "ach", is *brother, half-brother, relative, kin, same resemblance*. Hebrew 'men' means *portion* or *string of a harp*, from an unused root meaning *to apportion, to bestow*; it is related to 'mene', *number, apportion, ordain, mina, sixty shekels* and to 'min', *comparison, similar*. Also bearing in mind the importance of poetic devices, it should be noted that 'minchach', *gift*, is based on a rearrangement of letters.

Ahiman's brother, Sheshay or Sheshai, has a name that may mean *noble*, probably from Shashay, which is probably in turn from *bleached white, alabaster, fine linen*. However, 'shay' means *gift*, so this would neatly fit one possible meaning of Ahiman, *my brother is a gift*.

Talmay (Talmai) is the most interesting of the three names. I regard it as the likely source of Thomas. Talmai is said to mean *furrowed* from 'telem', *furrow, to accumulate (wealth)*. Talmai starts with the Hebrew letter tav. And although 'telem', *oppression* or *break up violently* starts with the Hebrew letter tet, I consider they have become so entangled that the names Talmon, *oppressor*, and Ptolemy, *aggressive, war-like*, both come from it. And thus, ultimately the Biblical names Bartholomew and Thomas both go back to Talmai, the one who caused doubt. Ironically, both Bartholomew and Thomas are remembered for not causing doubt, but having doubts.

See *God's Pageantry: The Threshold Guardians and the Covenant Defender* for an analysis of the name Thomas and its relationship to Talmai, one of the giants of Hebron.

27 Isaac Mozeson in *The Word: The Dictionary That Reveals The Hebrew Source of English* suggests that *neck* is derived from the same source as Anak.

28 See Exodus 24:9-11 and Exodus 32:1-25

29 There are many possible good choices. Begin your adventure by praying to God and asking Him to lead you to the right mentor, the right spiritual director or the right ministry—to a place where you'll find both real grace and light; not cheap grace or soft light. Grace that challenges you to wholeness, rather than lets you 'off the hook', and light that is surgical and healing.

30 The word *envy* comes from the Latin 'invidere' meaning *to look at with malice*. It's far worse than saying: 'I wish I had what you've got.' Malice is indicative of a feeling of hostility that says: 'I'm angry with you because of what you've got.' And anger, as Jesus pointed out, is murder of the heart. In addition, envy says to God: 'You got it wrong! You should have given me what he's got. I deserve better! You aren't providing for me as You should.'

Dig even a little below the surface of jealousy and envy, and it's obvious that they are attitudes of hatred towards others, as well as lack of trust in God along with ingratitude towards Him.

31 In *Poet & Peasant and Through Peasant Eyes: A Literary-Cultural Approach to the Parables in Luke*, Ken Bailey looks at the Aramaic translations of the gospels and points out that the original words of Jesus are profound, memorable and superbly poetic. It makes perfect sense to him why the gospel writers could have recalled the parables decades later and wrote them down. Minor variations in wording are the result of their pick of language options as they translated His parables into Greek.

32 Ephesians 2:10 in the Greek says, '*We are His poetry,*' rather than the usual rendering: '*We are His workmanship.*'

33 In Genesis 25:30, Esau asks Jacob not for *stew* or *lentils*, but for 'red'. The New American Standard Bible therefore translates his request as being for 'red stuff'. It is implied in this verse that the selling of his birthright involved a name covenant, since Esau acquires the name Edom, *red*.

34　Isaiah 30:7

35　Though, just to confuse the issue, this is often translated *authorities* while *powers* is used for *world-rulers*.

36　A unique word, 'kosmokrátor', *world powers* or *world-rulers*, is used in Ephesians 6:12 where, it seems, that Paul is making a hierarchical distinction between principalities, powers and world-rulers. Kosmokrátor derives from kosmos, *world, universe, cosmos* and from krátos, *strength, might, dominion, power* or from krateó, *rule, master, control*.

37　http://nbcnews.to/2rAqXB2

38　Also sometimes **pht**, as in the name Napthali, *twisting, wrestling, cunning*.

39　Another name for the moon goddesses, Roman Diana or Greek Selene, used in Ben Jonson's *Cynthia's Revels* or *The Fountain of Selfe-Love*.

40　Rilian's mother throughout the *Narnia* series never receives any name beyond Ramandu's Daughter. However, in *The Silver Chair*, she is very much like Herodis, the Eurydice-figure in *Sir Orfeo*. Unfortunately, unlike the medieval tale, there's no happy ending for her.

41　It's difficult to know what Lewis intended Harfang to mean but 'har' is so often, across so many languages, associated with high places, I'm assuming it's simply *high*. And 'fang' might be a *pointy tooth* but I doubt that's sufficient for Lewis the wordmaster. How about from 'fane', *temple*? The oracular shrine at Delphi was both high on a cliff and in an underground cave. Harfang, as a high castle and threshold to the Underworld, fits both.

42　Prince Caspian is a decidedly unusual name. It could be inspired by the Caspian Sea, or come from the Jewish word, 'caspi', *silver* or Old Persian, 'caspar', *treasurer* or from 'casapi', *butcher*. Perhaps it's most likely to be Persian since Caspian's uncle, Miraz, seems to have a name derived from 'mirza', Persian for *prince*.

43　The Janissary spirit is not discussed at length in this present book. In brief, it is an army spirit whose main agenda is to turn children against their parents. Specifically, it wants the son to kill the father. Its secondary agenda is to get its enemies to provide all the resources necessary for the war against themselves. The work of this spirit is found in 2 Samuel 2:8–28 where it is revealed as a threshold guardian (though not by this name) and is also shown to be in alliance with a vampire spirit. For more information, see *God's Pottery: The Sea of Names and the Pierced Inheritance*, Armour Books 2016

44 abarim-publications.com/Meaning/Talmai.html

45 This part-human, part-goat creature from classical mythology became associated with Morris dancing—no doubt due to the fact the performers often wore animal masks and costumes so they seemed to be part-human, part-beast.

According to Robert Graves in *The White Goddess*, Morris dancing had its origins in a fertility rite which culminated in the sacrificial death of one of the dancers. This victim was often called 'Robin'. The slayer was often called 'Jack'. During the orgiastic festivities, the masked Morris dancers took as many women to bed as they wished. Nine months later, a woman might call her child Robinson (*Robin's son*) or Jackson (*Jack's son*), if she knew the identity of the father. Or, if the night had been dark and she wasn't sure who she'd been with, she might just call her child Morrison (*son of a Morris dancer*).

Although it is never mentioned by name, there are faint echoes of Morris dancing ceremonies throughout *The Lion, The Witch and the Wardrobe*. In some Morris dancing traditions, a piece of currant cake or confectionary is impaled on a sword and distributed to the onlookers. Sometimes the sword-bearer would be a Queen dressed in white—her name, if she was not anonymous, often being Maid Marian. This modern practice echoes an ancient and barbaric practice: originally it was a human head impaled on the sword.

In *The Lion, the Witch and the Wardrobe*, the White Witch, the self-styled Queen of Narnia, tempts Edmund with Turkish Delight. That sugary confection symbolises 'the head of my enemy'. No wonder Edmund can't get enough!

46 Jill Pole has a surname redolent of the World Ash Tree, the centre of the realms of the gods and of mankind's 'Middle Earth' in Norse mythology. It also evokes the 'axis mundi', the axis of the world, as well as the ideas of north pole, polestar, cynosure and cosmic mountain.

Her first name recalls the girl in the nursery rhyme, *Jack and Jill*. This verse is considered by folklorists to be a fragment of the tale of Hjúki and Bil—thought to be asteroids captured in lunar orbit which eventually were pulled into earth's gravity and splashed down into the sea. (Lewis Spence, *Dictionary of Non-Classical Mythology*)

47 For many years, the story floated around that Lewis had likely seen a packet of Aslans—Turkish cigarettes with a picture of a lion on the front. However, Kathryn Lindskoog maintained that Lewis would have known the word from the thesis of MA Manzalaoui, whose work on the *Arabian Nights* he supervised from 1945–48. While this may explain the provenance of a word meaning *lion*, it doesn't account for the divine character of Aslan.

My belief is that we have to head further north into the Scandinavian languages to make that connection. Lewis confessed that from an early age he was 'crazed with northern-ness'—obsessed with the stories of the Norse gods. It all started for him with a retelling of the death of Balder in a story called *Tegna's Drapa*.

This description of a high and lonely echo, throbbing across arctic skies, ignited his imagination. For me, its obvious culmination was in the endless winter of *The Lion, the Witch and the Wardrobe* which is so much like the enchanted fimbulwinter of Norse mythology. In addition, several significant names come from Norse mythology (Fenris Ulf in the US edition who is the wolf Maugrim in the British version; and of course the World Ash Tree.)

Lewis' admiration for all things northern was so well-known that he was the natural choice during the Second World War for an unusual mission through the Secret Intelligence Service: convince the people of Iceland that Britain's surprise invasion of their country wasn't the action of an enemy. Win the hearts of the people so that they would be on-side and would help against any German naval operations in the North Atlantic. In this propaganda broadcast, Lewis spoke on 'The Norse Spirit in English Literature', explaining that he addressed the people of Iceland to repay a great debt. His imaginative life, so he said, was awakened at the age of 14 by Norse mythology and his love of it had deepened when he began to study the Icelandic language at Oxford.

With all this in mind, I feel that any analysis of the name Aslan that ignores the Old Norse/Old Icelandic language is not doing justice to Lewis' first literary love.

So, what does Aslan mean in Old Norse? Simply *god of the land*. The first syllable 'as' is *god*, while the final syllable 'lan' comes from *land*.

God of the land is perfect description of the Lord of the Wood and the Great King of Narnia. Fortuitously, Aslan is a word that can cross languages and still retain a valid meaning.

48 I don't know whether this is a personal discovery or whether I read it somewhere. My sincere apologies if I have used this information without attribution. It will be corrected in later editions.

49 This is, of course, similar to Persephone, the goddess of autumn winds and Queen of the Underworld. There is a possibility that the Autumn Feast of the giants may be influenced by those winds. However, despite this and despite the fact Persephone was said to have a silver chair, I still think the weight of allusion in *The Silver Chair* points far more to the Pythia than to Hades' consort.

The Mother's Blessing and God's Favour Towards Women

Each book in this series can be read independently.

The first volume, *More Precious than Pearls*, highlights the admiration of many Jewish writers for the women of the Exodus. They were remarkable women of steadfast, tested faith: armour-bearers, watchmen, game-changers, gatekeepers and cupbearers.

The second volume, *As Resplendent as Rubies*, explores the role of Biblical women who were kingmakers, visionaries, navigators, sentinels, mentors, culture-changers and even God-namers.

This third volume, *As Exceptional as Sapphires*, is about the women builders—the purveyors and chamberlains, nation-shapers, torch-bearers and paradigm-shifters.

The gifts and offices of God are irrevocable, so it is wise to learn the Scriptural principles behind these divine appointments as we seek to live out the call of God on our lives.

Jesus and the Healing of History

The patterns of the past are locked into the landscape. People need healing, but so does the land. Every location mentioned in the ministry of Jesus is profoundly significant. Where a placename is revealed in relation to the healing of a person, then—if it is possible to examine the background of that place— we realise that people, land and history are simultaneously being healed.

When Jesus went to Sychar and met the woman at the well, He went to the specific location where the kingdom passed down from David was ripped in two. And in being proclaimed 'the Messiah', He reunited the divided kingdom. Five momentous covenants were enacted at this place, so it is no wonder a five-times-married woman represents its history.

Jesus and the Healing of History is a series that delves into the background of the localities where Jesus performed His miracles. Each book is lavishly illustrated in full-colour.

Strategies for the Threshold

(See overleaf for description)

#1 Dealing with Python: Spirit of Constriction
#2 Dealing with Ziz: Spirit of Forgetting
#3 Name Covenant: Invitation to Friendship
#4 Hidden in the Cleft: True and False Refuge
#5 Dealing with Leviathan: Spirit of Retaliation
#6 Dealing with Resheph: Spirit of Trouble
#7 Dealing with Azazel: Spirit of Rejection

The books in this series all deal with different and significant aspects of thresholds—which, in a spiritual sense, refer to the 'doorway' into our life's calling.

In summary, the obstacles are simply the *threefold guard:* the stone, the watch and the seal which were barriers to the resurrection of Jesus. Similar difficulties face us as we seek to move through the doorway into our calling.

The soldiers on watch are analogous to the threshold guardians—hostile spirits of great authority that seek to block our way into our destiny. Just as *love* overcomes the spirit of Python, so there's another specific Fruit of the Spirit to overcome each different threshold guardian. The Fruit of the Spirit are not only the means of identifying fellow disciples of Christ, they are weapons in our fight for faith. Just as fruit was weaponised in the Garden of Eden, so now we have to mature the Fruit of the Spirit in our lives so it will be at our disposal when needed.

Where to start?

At the first volume and just work through? Of course, you could, but you'd just trace the author's line of thinking, rather than look for what the Holy Spirit wants to reveal to you. After lots of feedback from readers, most of them recommend starting with Book #4, *Hidden in the Cleft*. The legal power of the threshold guardians is bound up with covenant and, more particularly, with our agreement with ancestral covenants through 'false refuges'. Until we realise the subtle way these counterfeit havens operate in our lives, we won't get rid of them or deal with the associated idols and covenants.

Alternatively, you could simply start where you discern your own issue lies: is your life beset with forgetting? With retaliation? With rejection?

Forthcoming volumes are expected on the spirits of abuse and armies, as well as other threshold-related topics. Each book contains a final summary, plus sample prayers at the end of each chapter as prompts for intercession.

www.ingramcontent.com/pod-product-compliance
Lightning Source LLC
Chambersburg PA
CBHW052042280426
43661CB00085B/52